Winter Holiday Coloring Book

40 Beautiful holiday designs for coloring in

By Artist

Dwyanna Stoltzfus

Happy Holiday's
To you and yours!!

Copyright © 2016 by Dwyanna Stoltzfus

ALL RIGHTS RESERVED

ISBN-10:1541058674

ISBN-13:978-1541058675

About:

You are going to love this holiday coloring book!!

Get ready to color 40 beautiful winter themed doodle art coloring pages by Artist Dwyanna Stoltzfus.

The designs in this book are beautiful.

This wonderful holiday coloring book will provide many hours of entertainment.

It will also provide hours of peaceful

calm and relaxation away from the stress that often comes with the holidays.

In this adult coloring book you will find 40 beautiful illustrations, printed one per page.

This includes:

7 cupcake designs

8 Snowman designs

5 Snowflake designs

6 Stocking designs

7 Pages of 3-D stars that can be colored, cut out and folded to make a 3-D star

That can be hung on your tree. There are 4 sizes of stars. 20 stars total.

And a variety of 7 other holiday designs.

You can use this coloring book to help you relax and unwind or just to have fun.

You can color the illustrations simply or add depth by shading.

Crayons are not recommended for the intricate detail but can be used on some of the pages.

You can also color with fine tip markers, gel pens, and colored pencils.

Enjoy the experience of coloring!!

But most of all relax and have fun!!

Coloring tips:

If you desire to add depth to your coloring you can shade with colored pencils.

Use dark colors around edges and into the peaks. Blend in light colors for the

middle and more open spaces. You can use black to darken areas,

and white to lighten and brighten areas.

Acknowledgments

Thank You to my family for all your support
of my art and this project.
I could not have done it without you!!

Thank You God for the gift and love
Of art and drawing!!

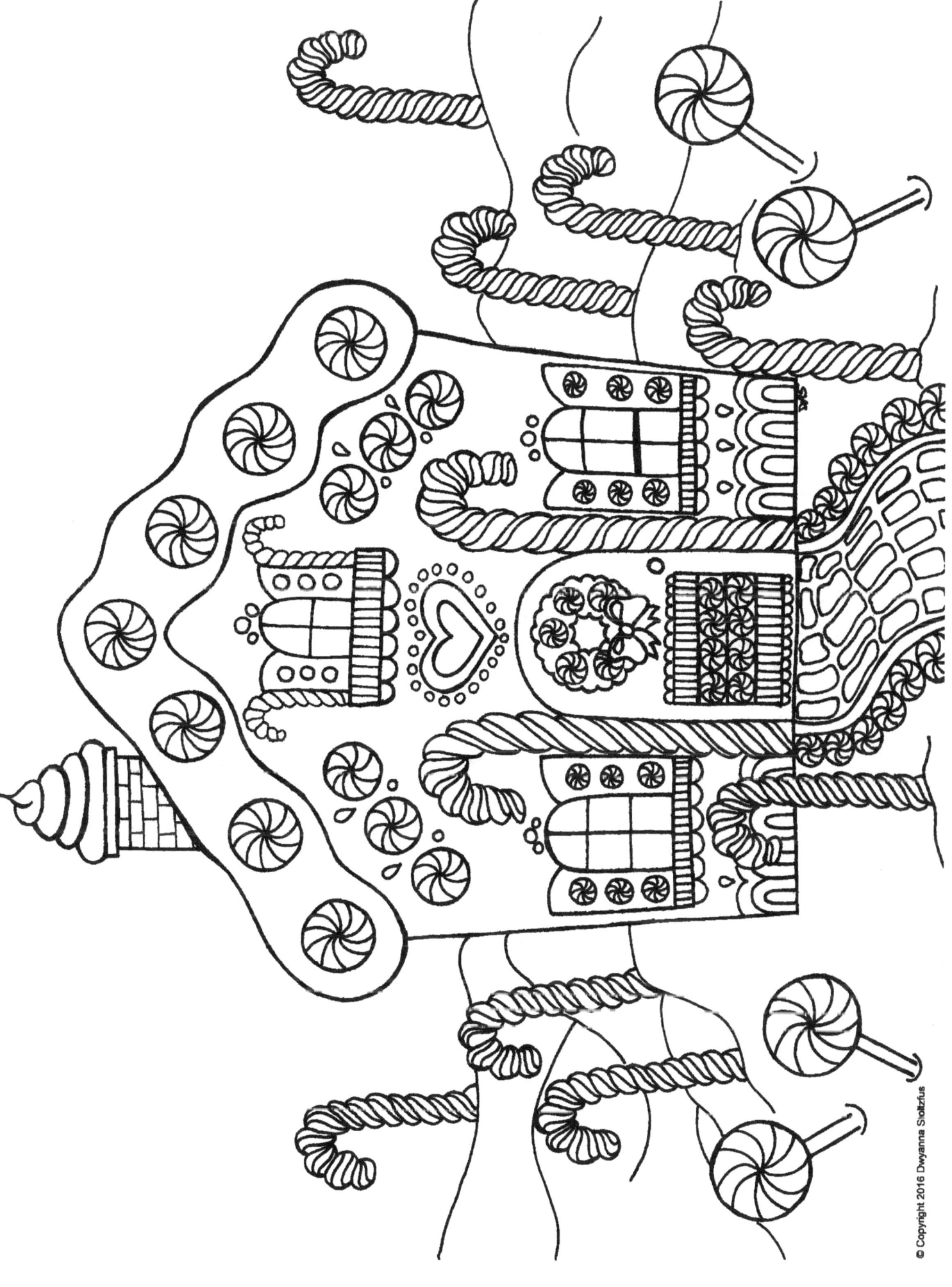

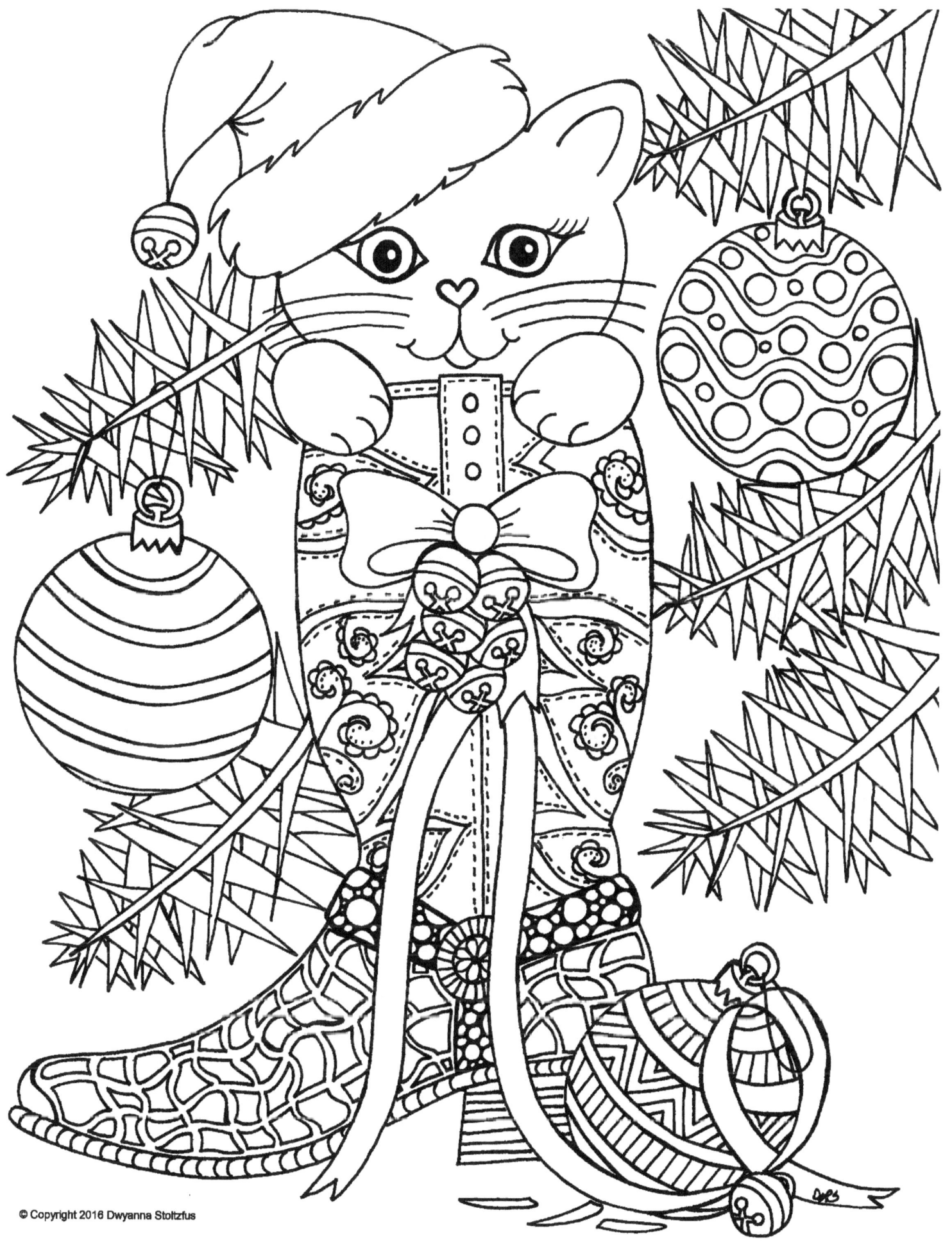

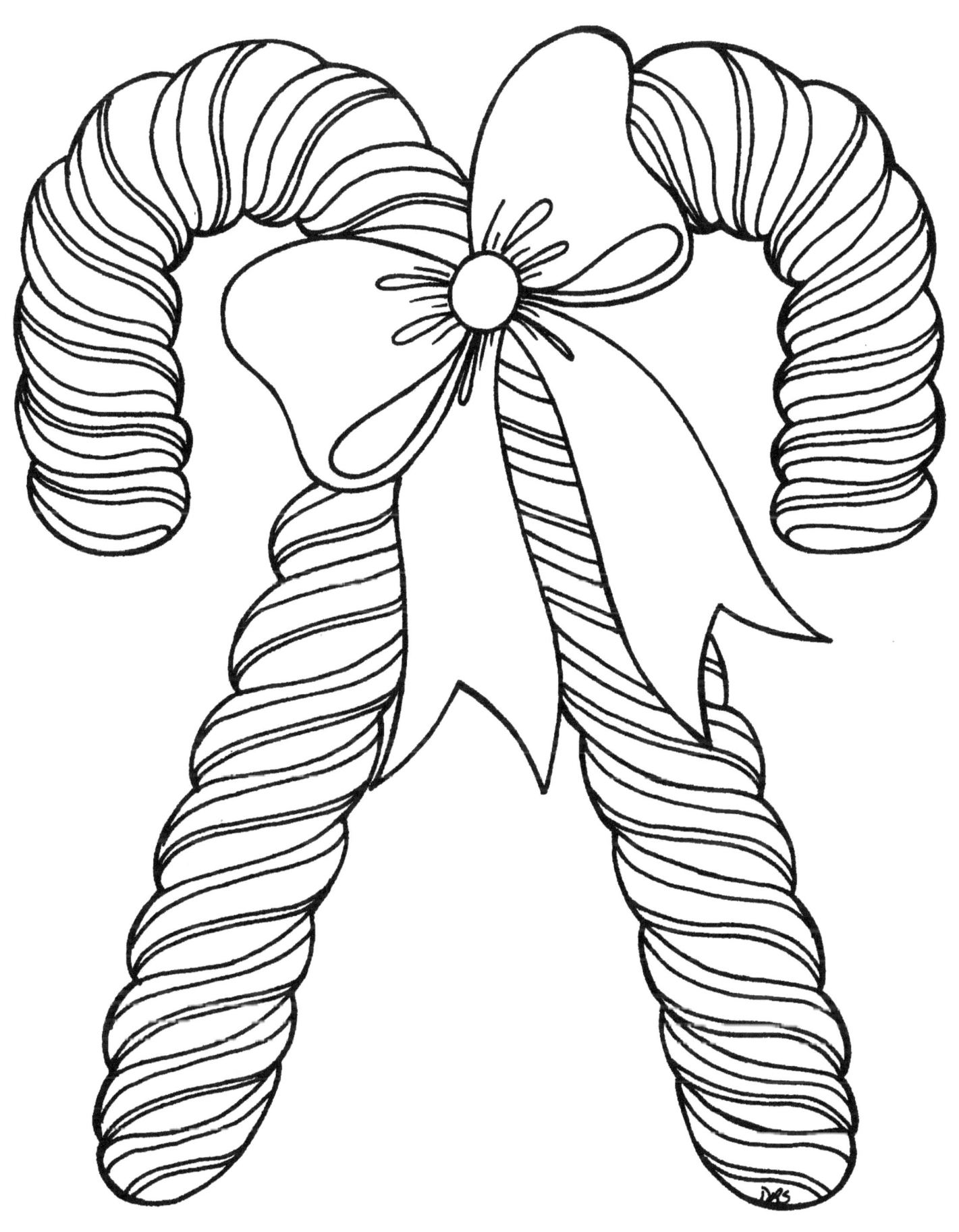

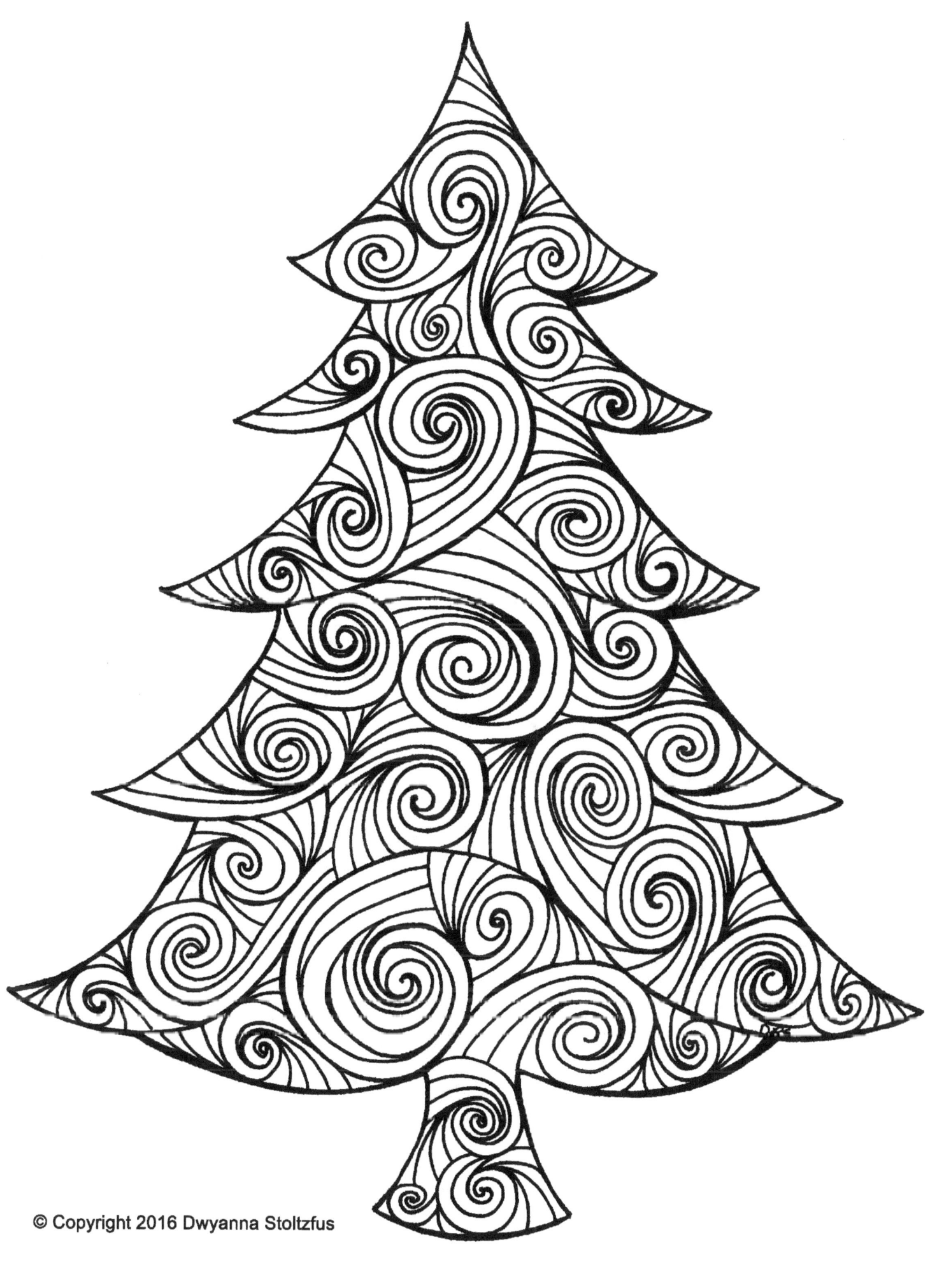

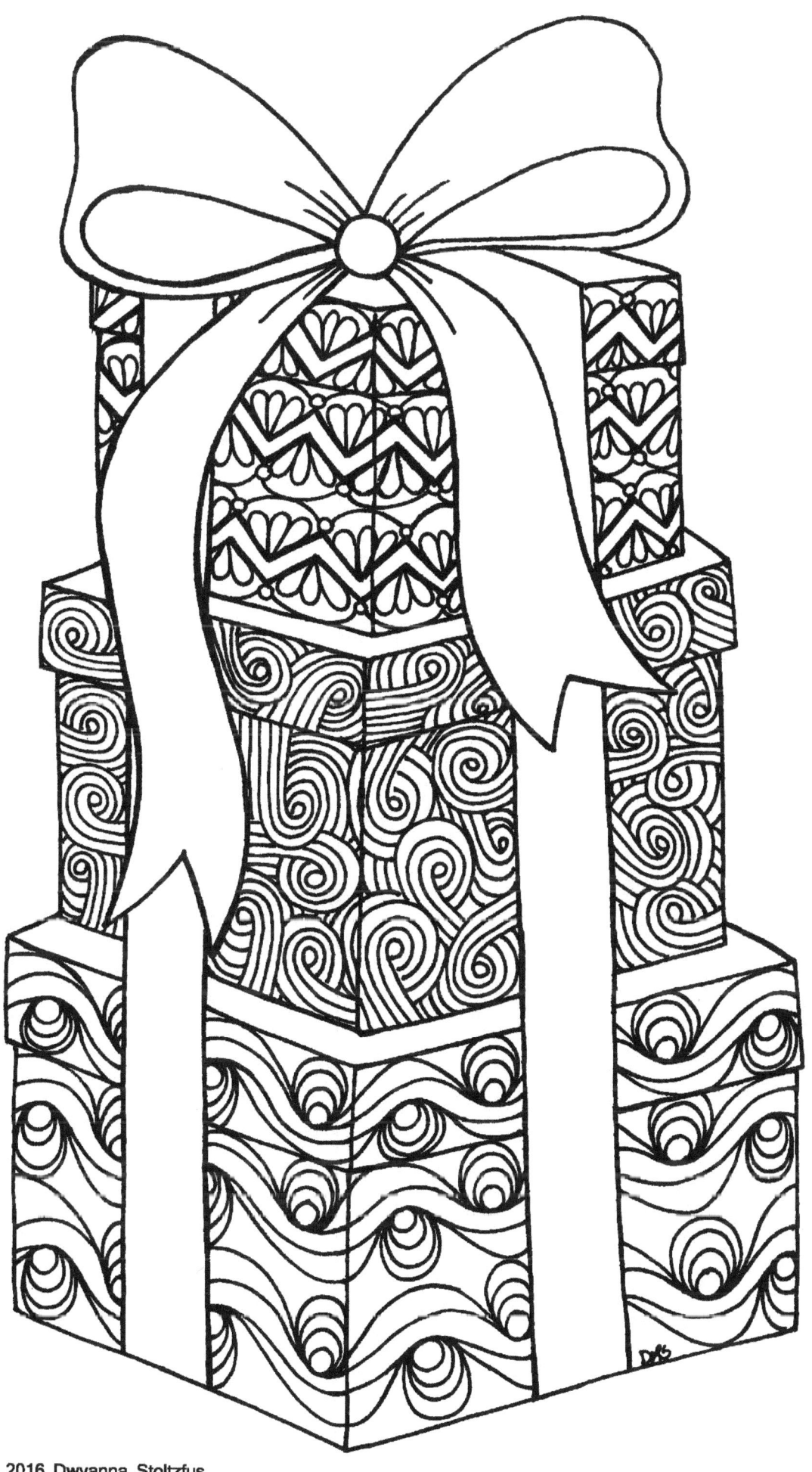

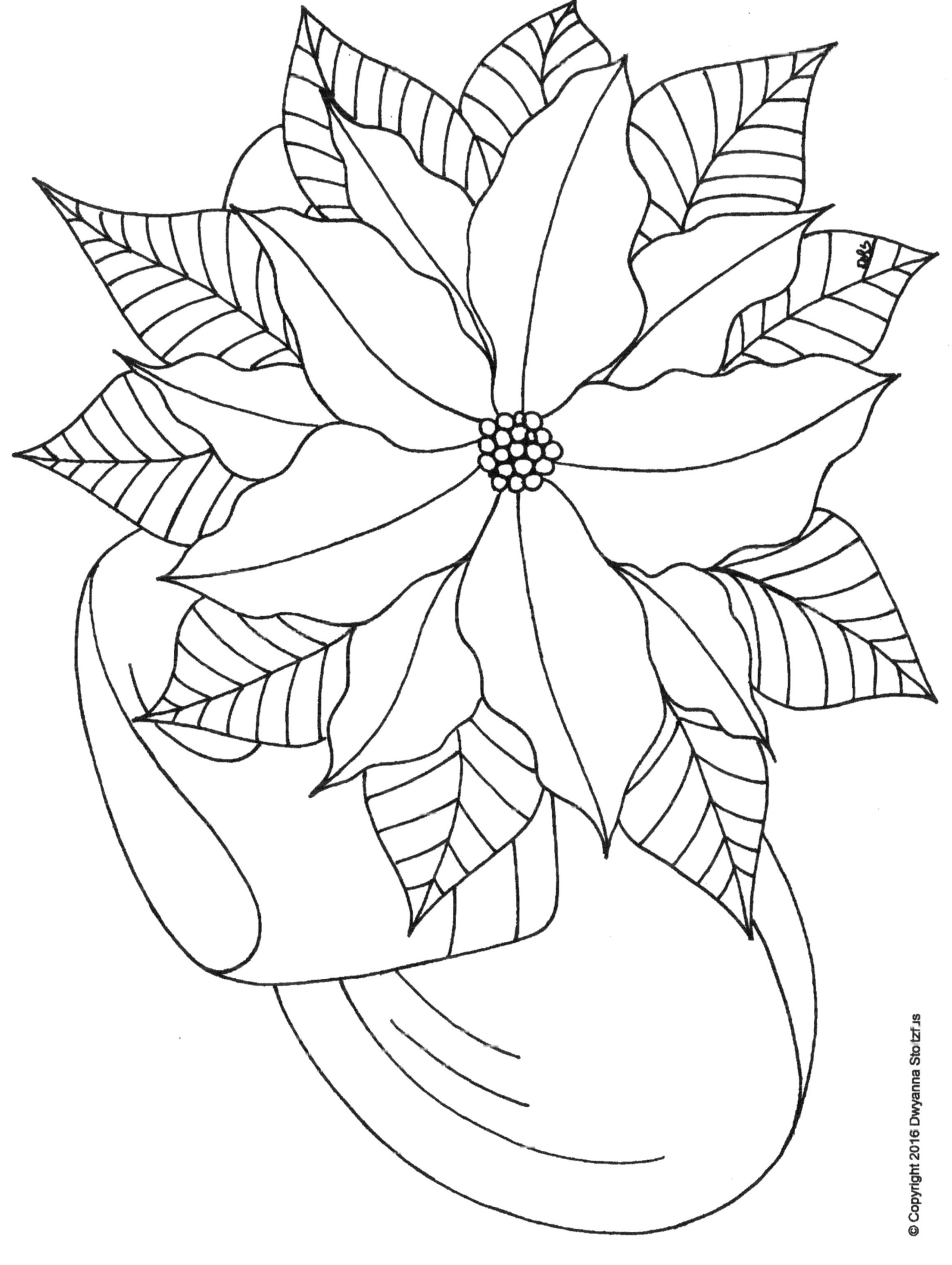

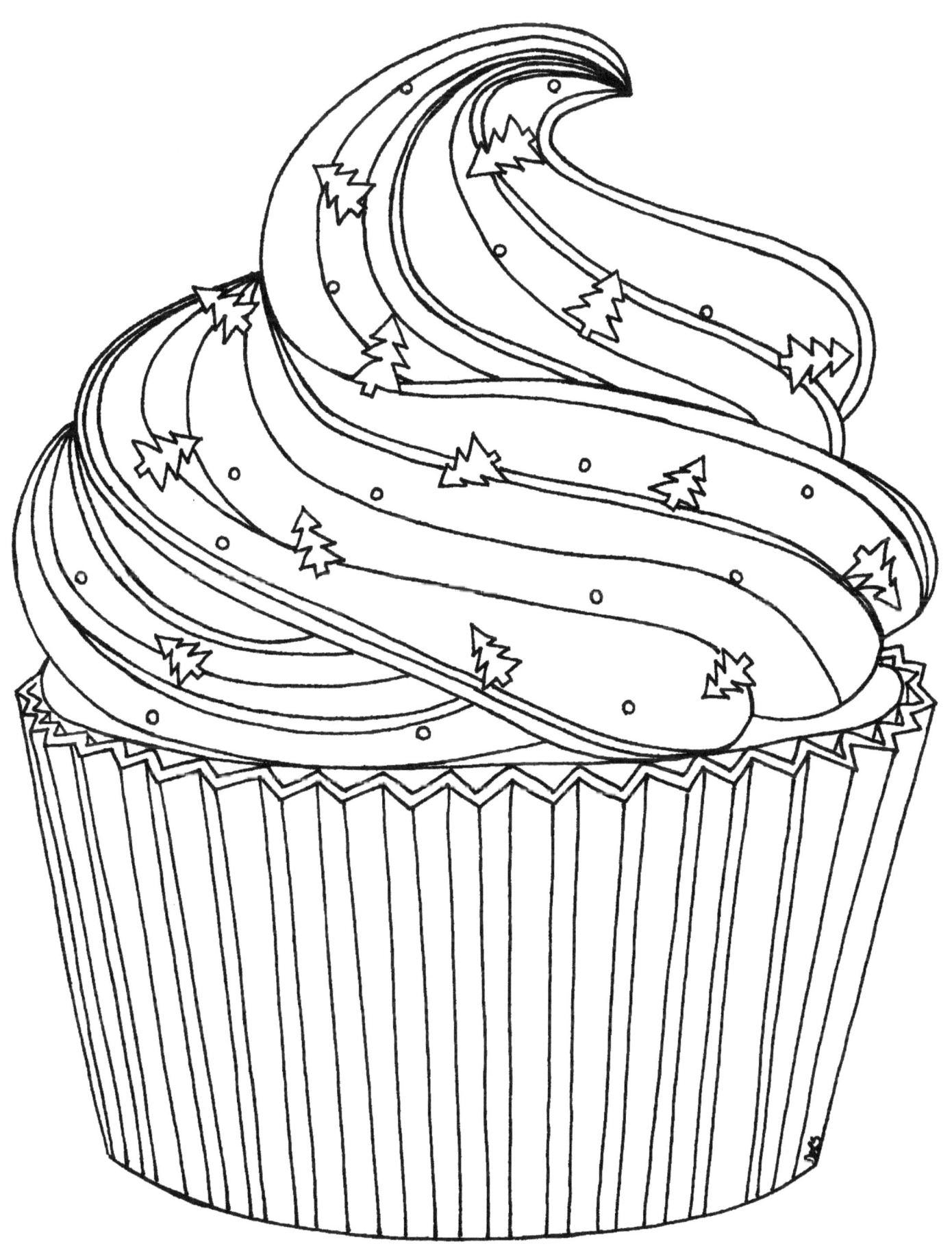

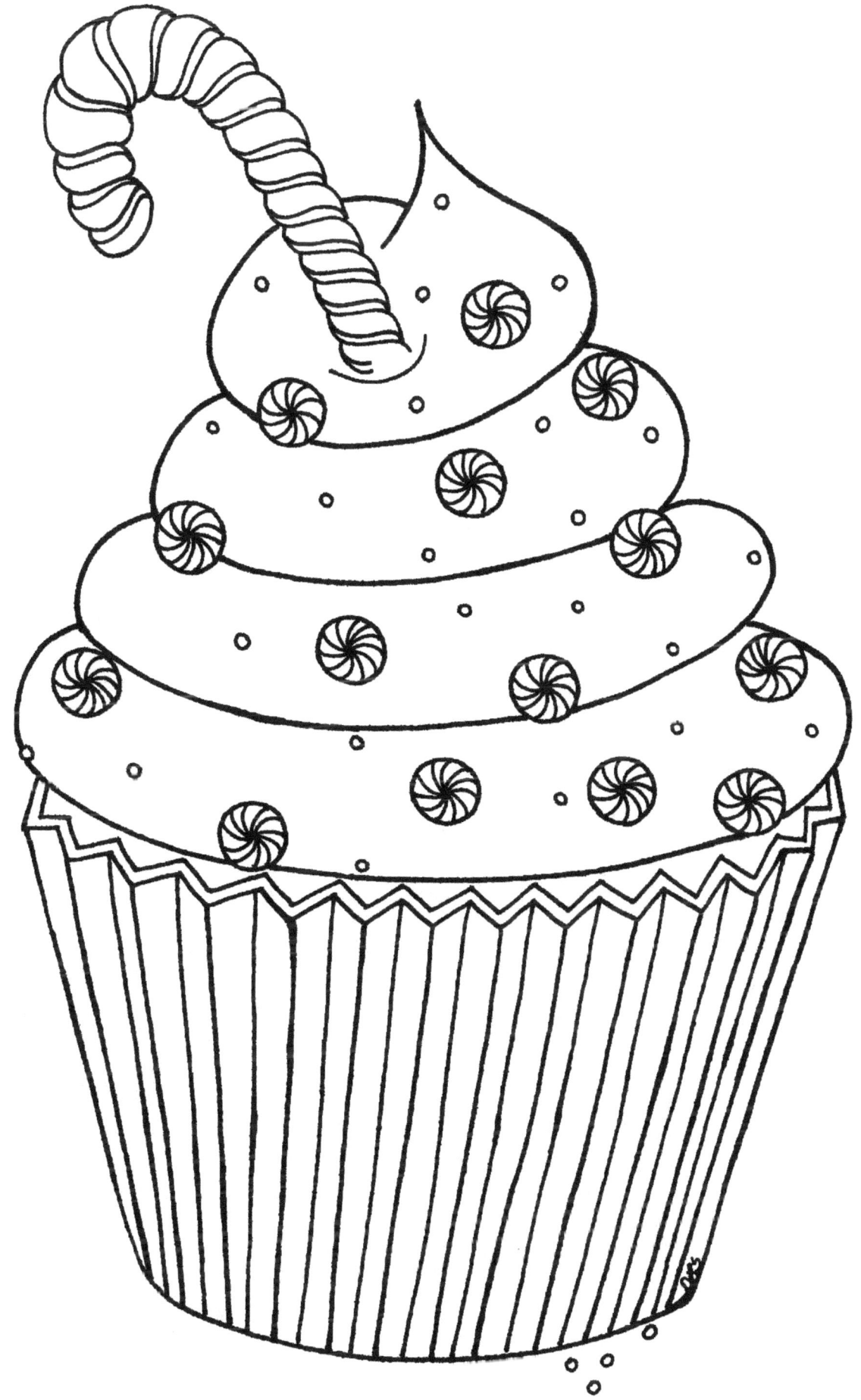

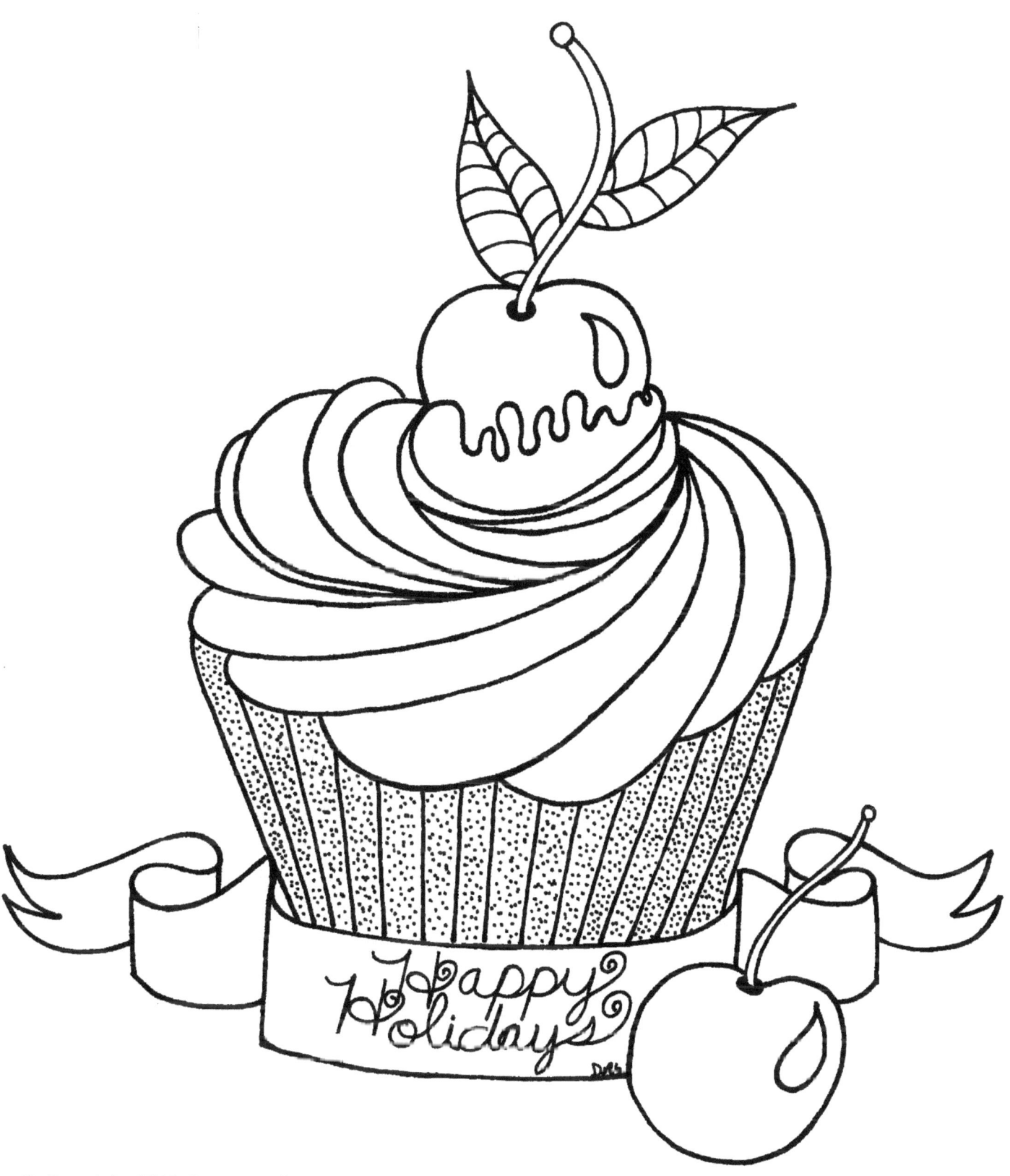

Happy Holidays

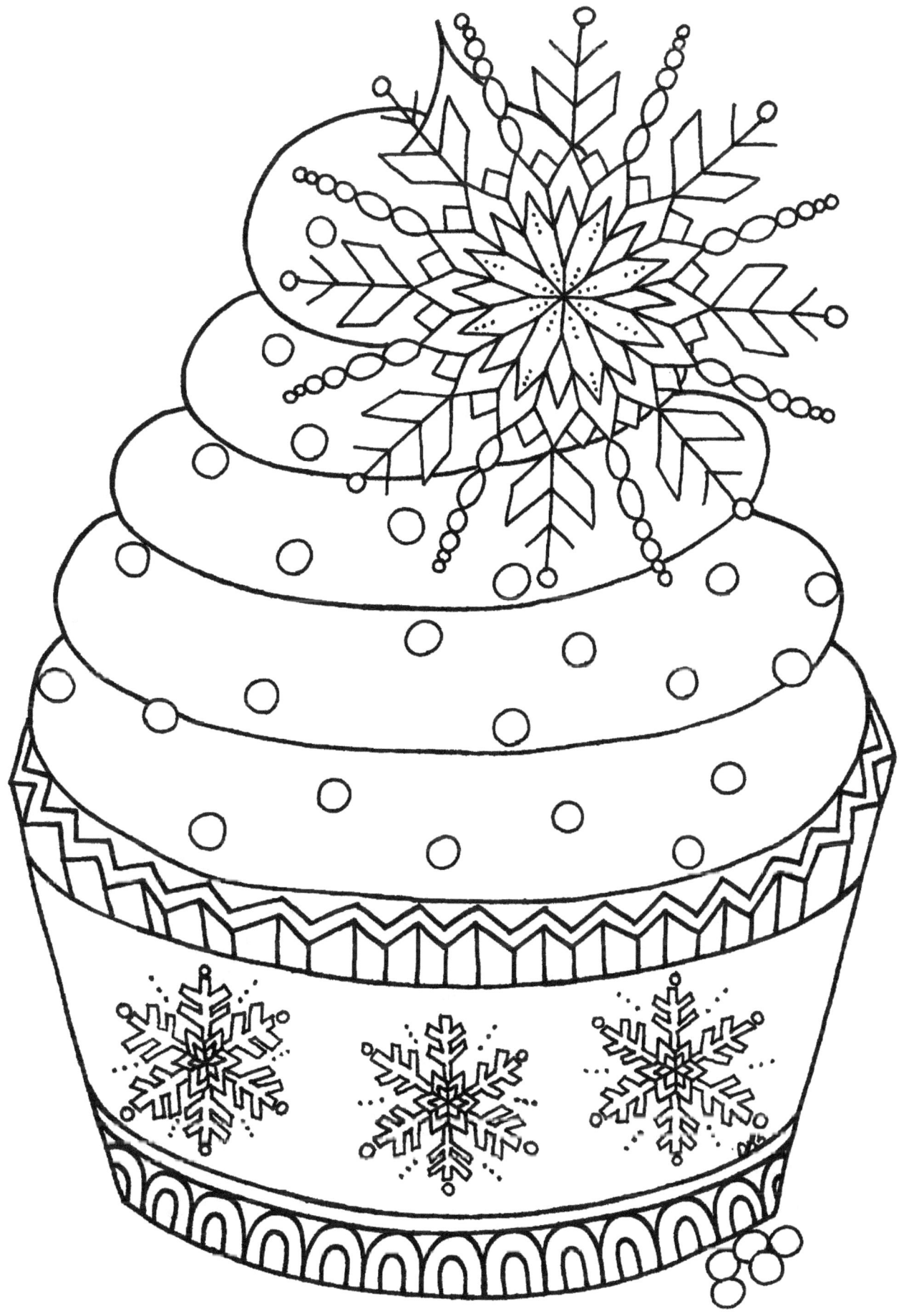

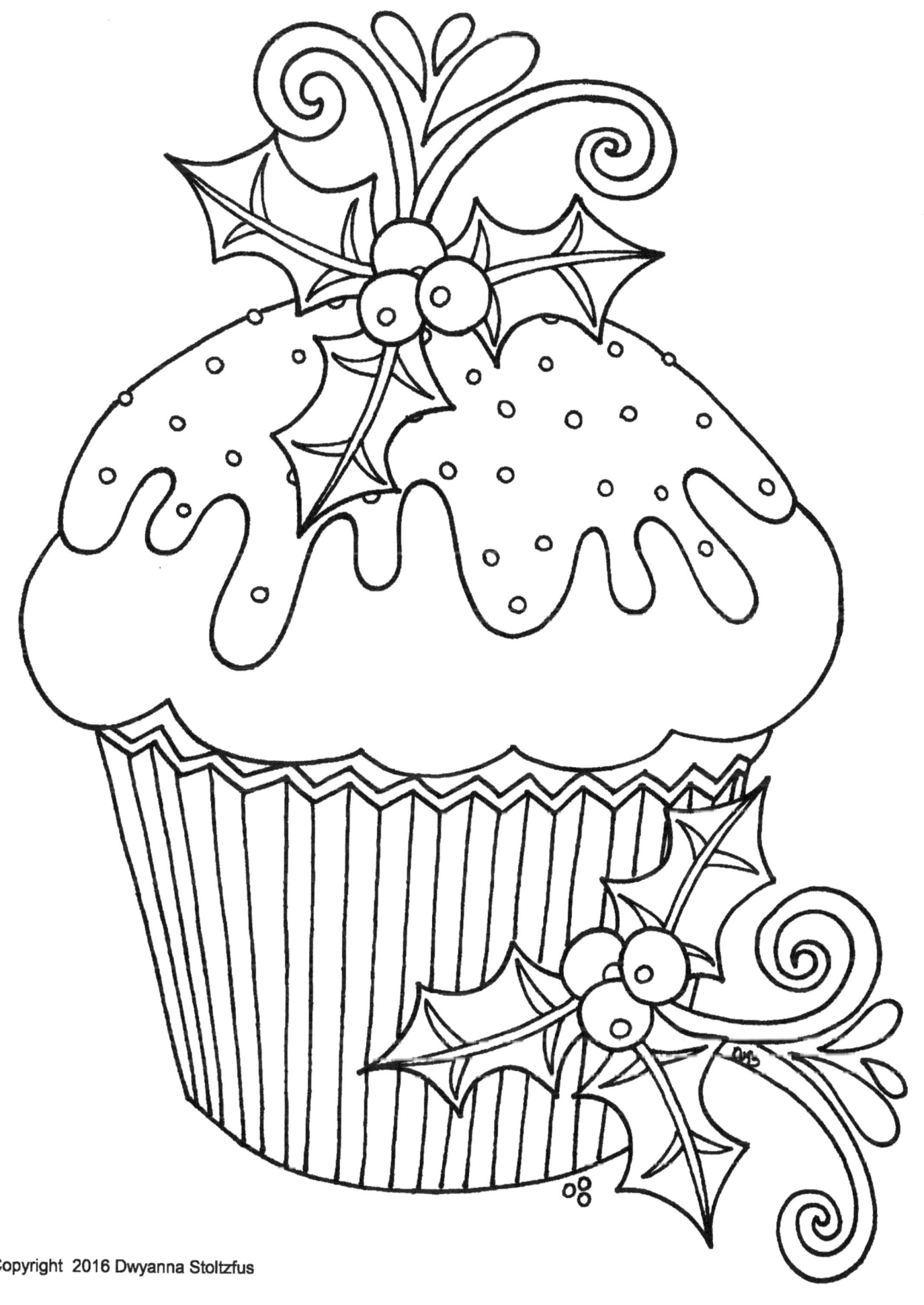

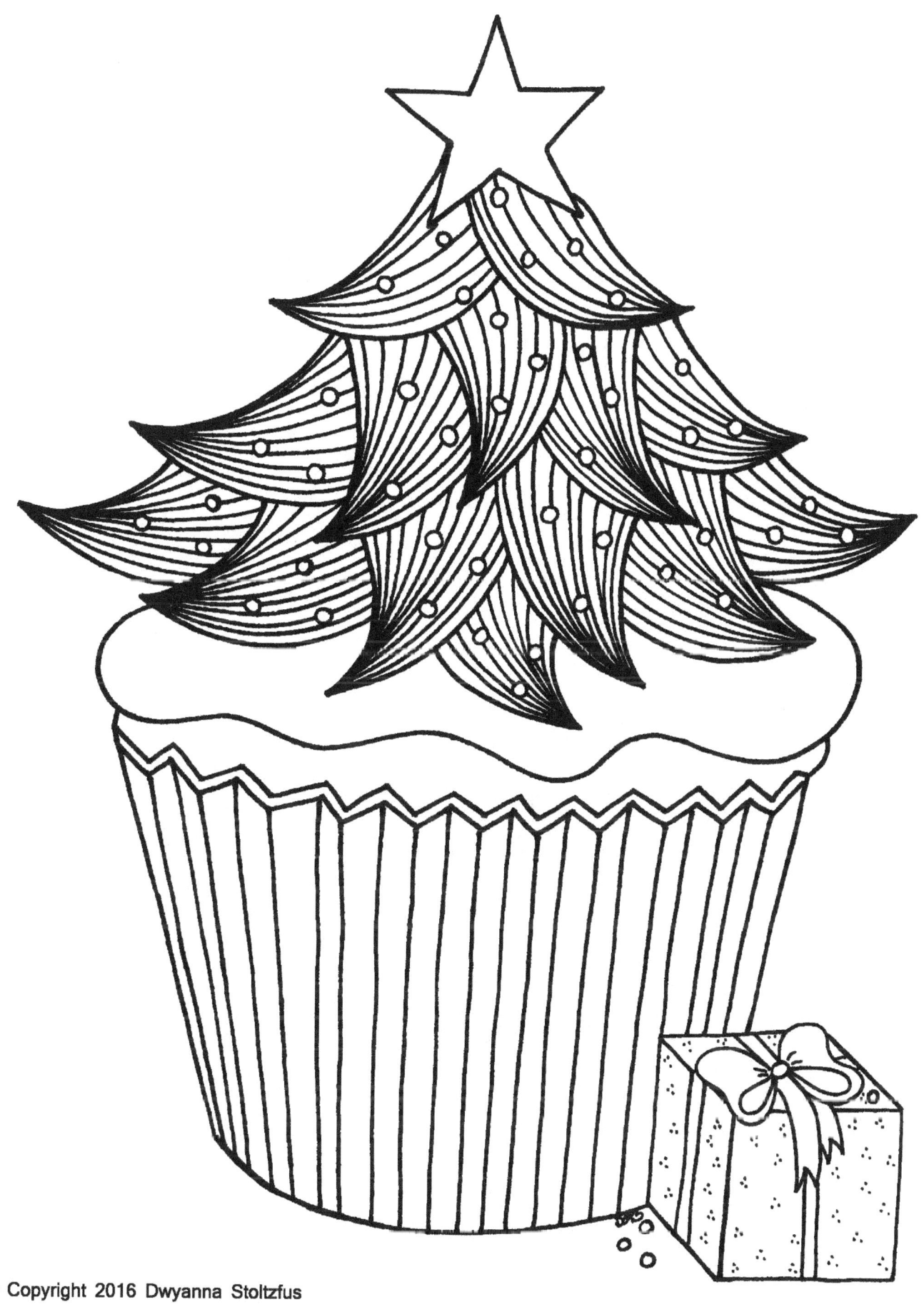

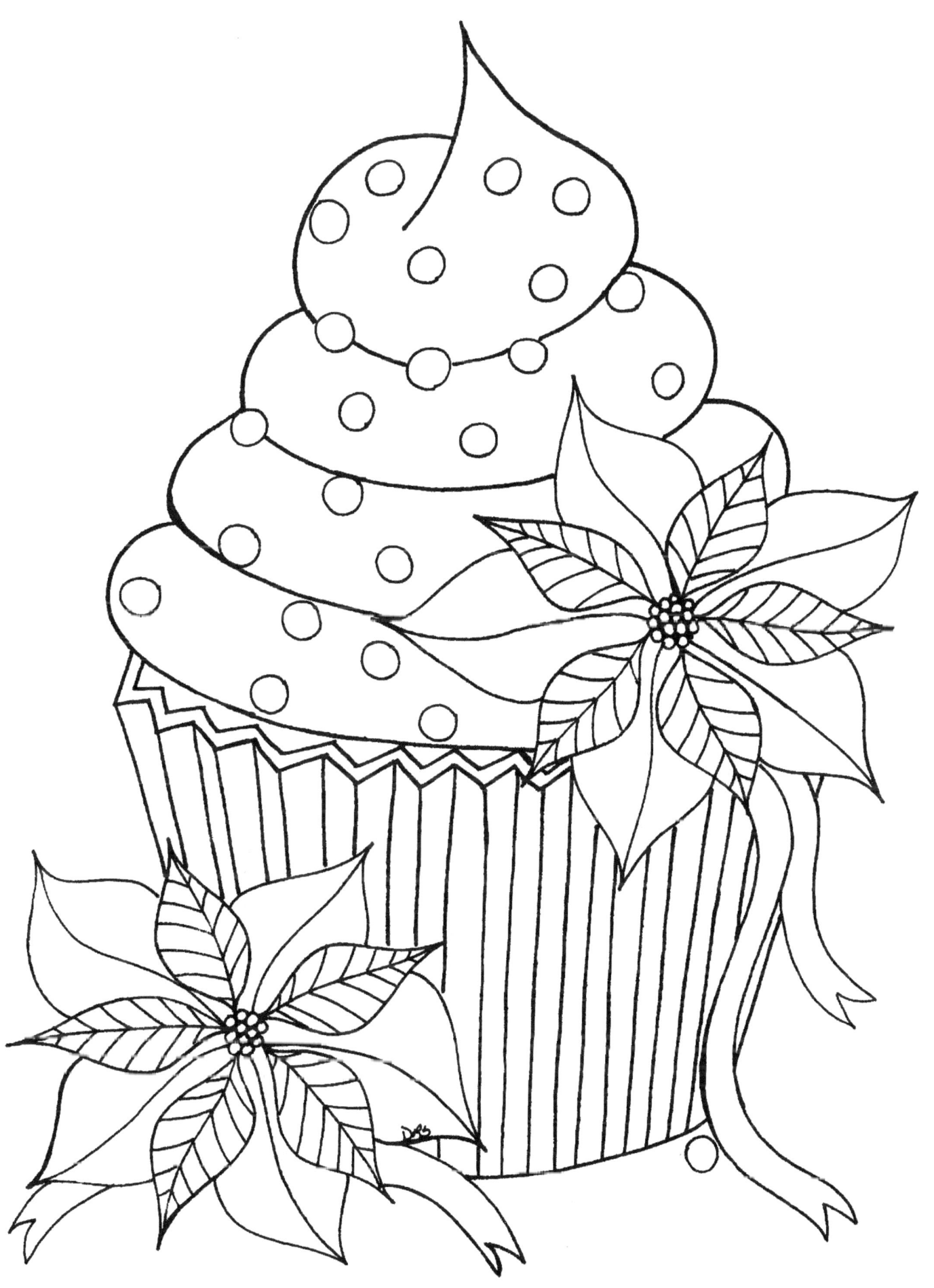

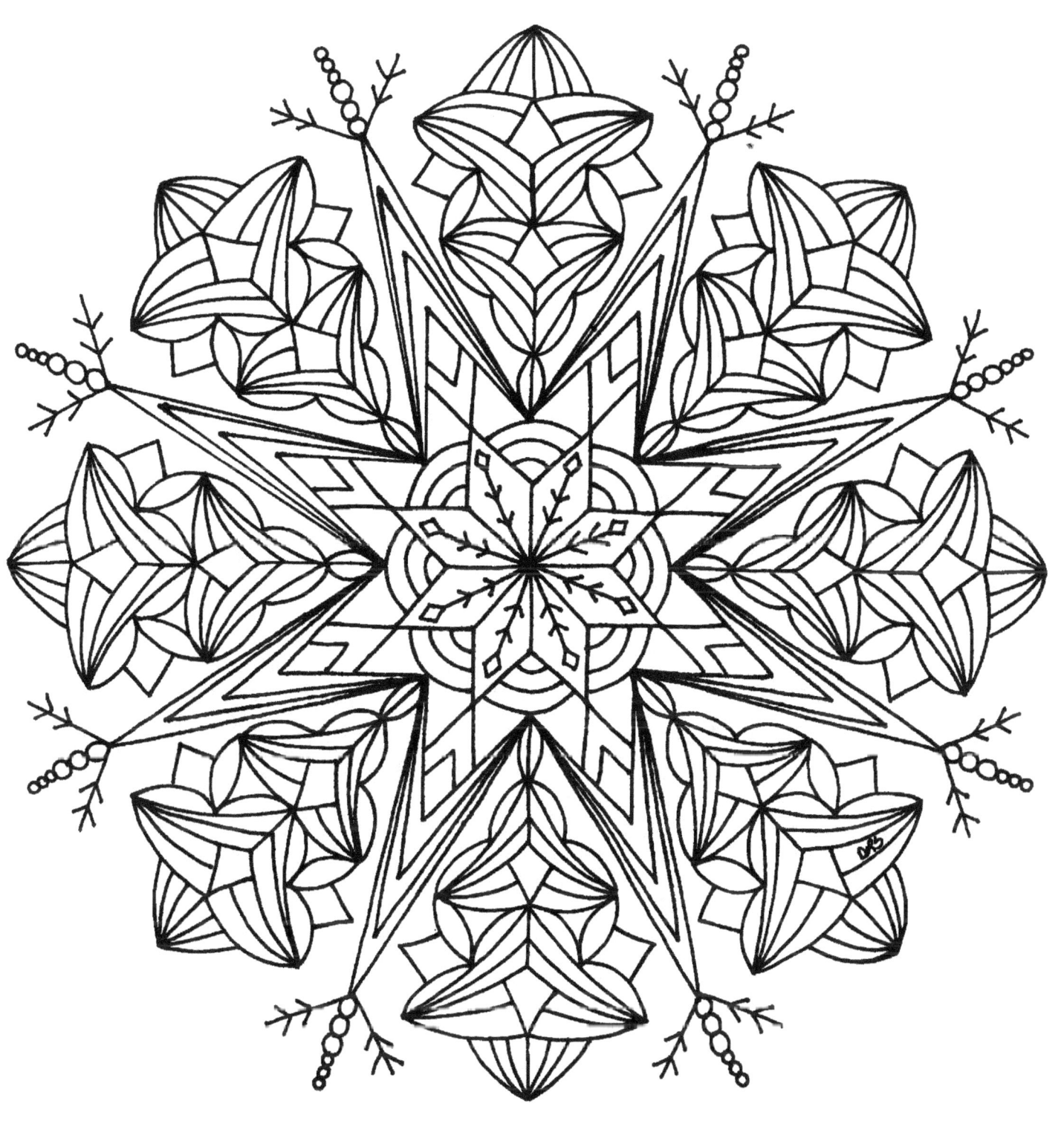

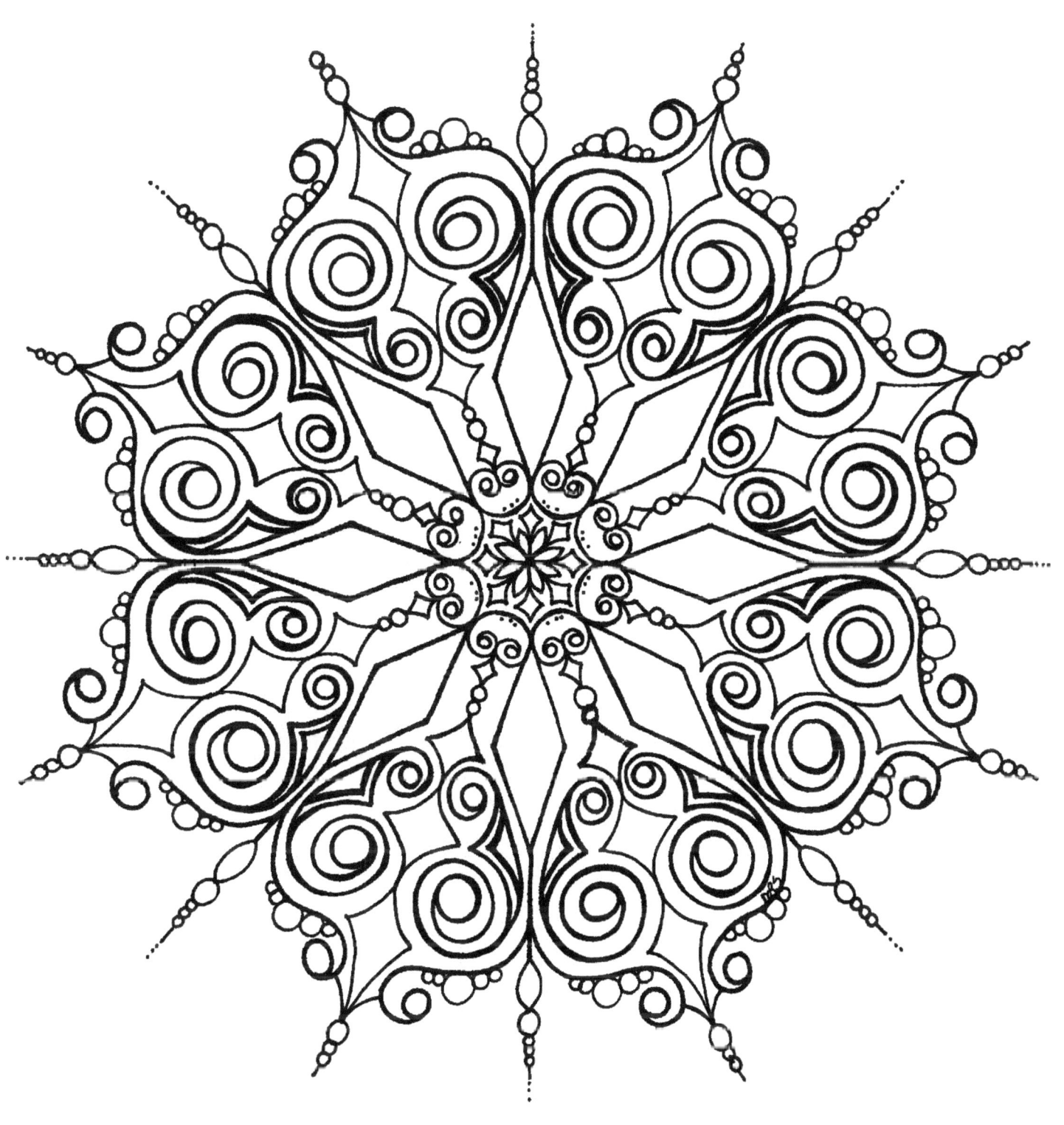

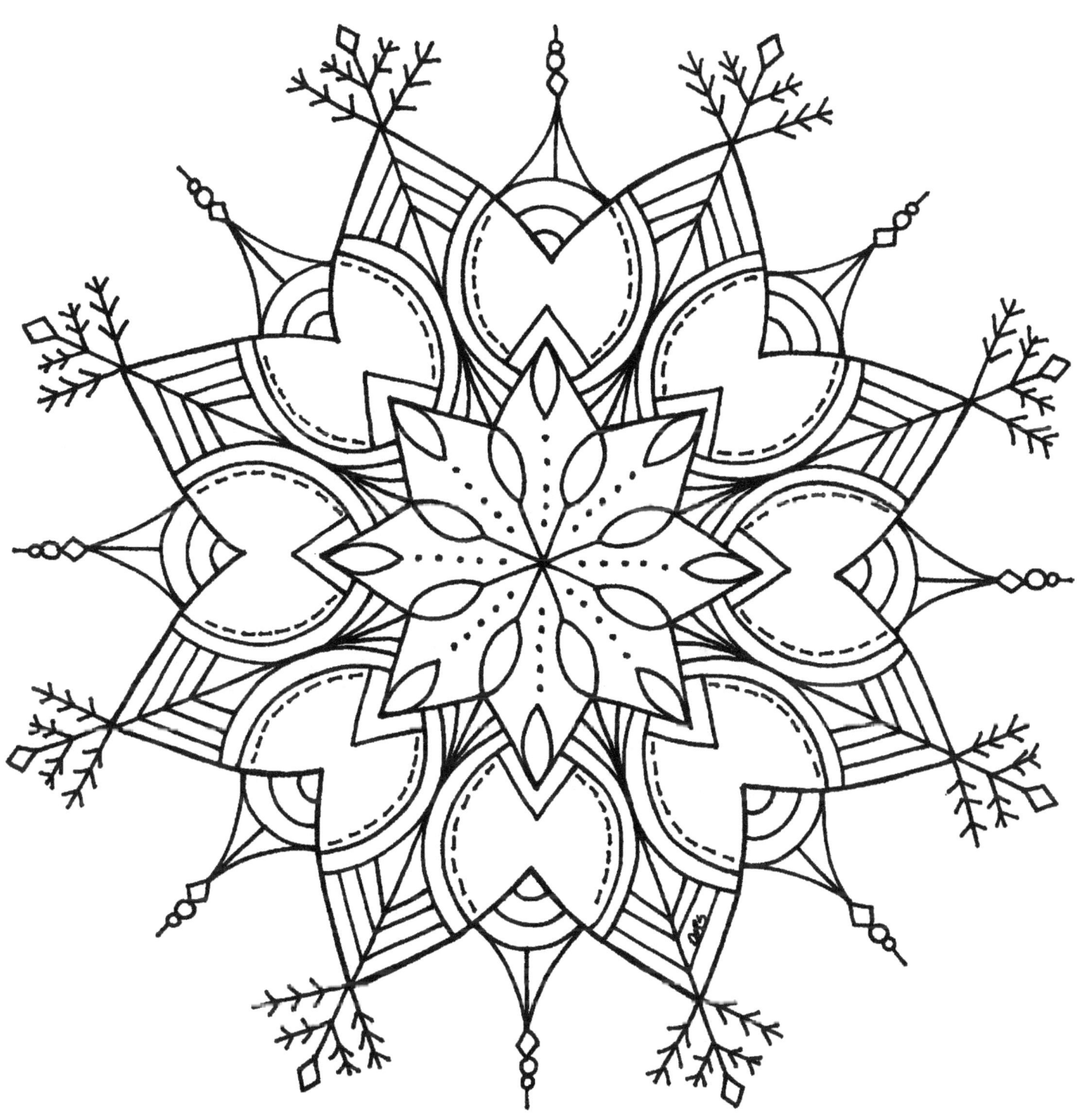

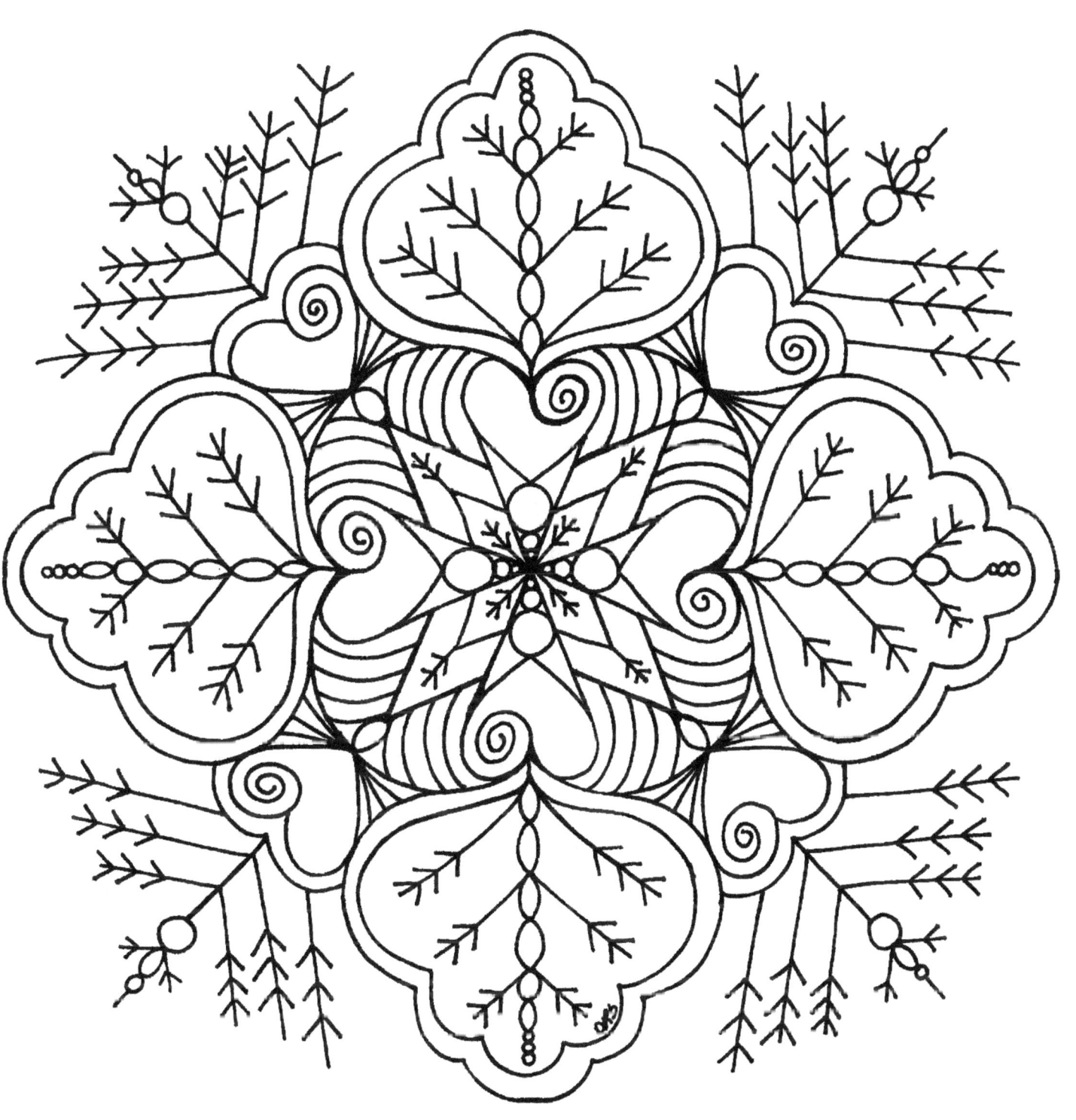

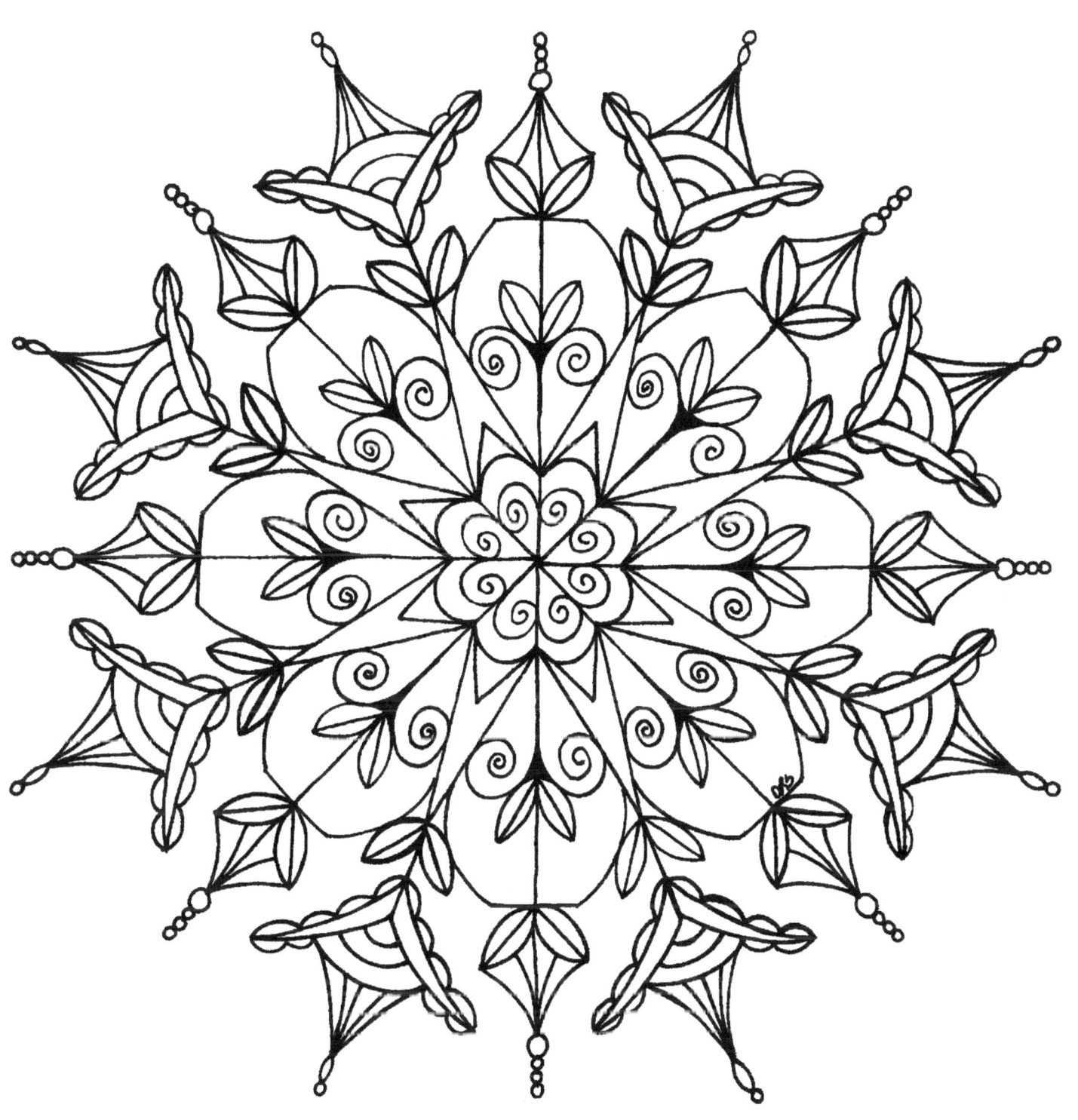

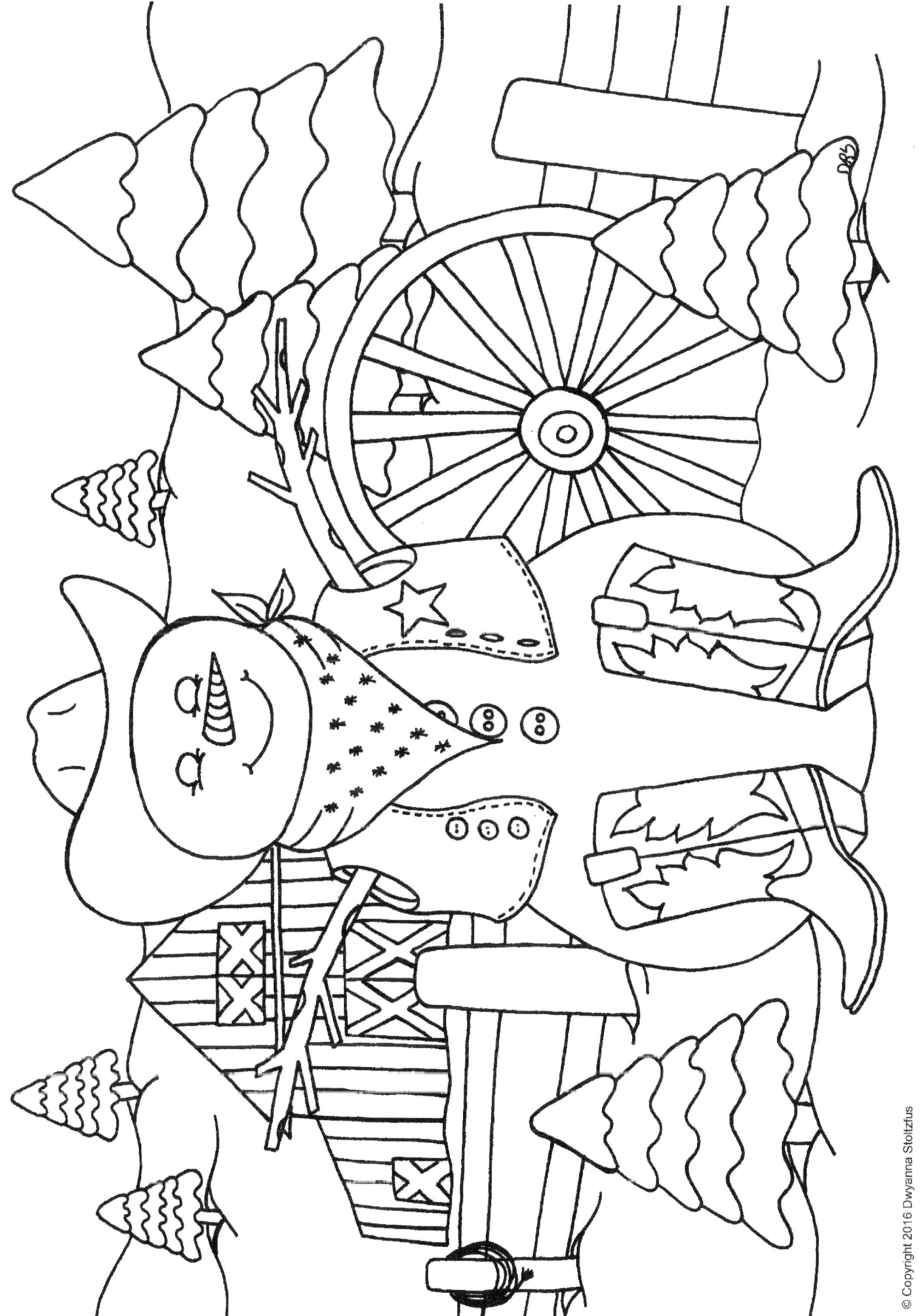

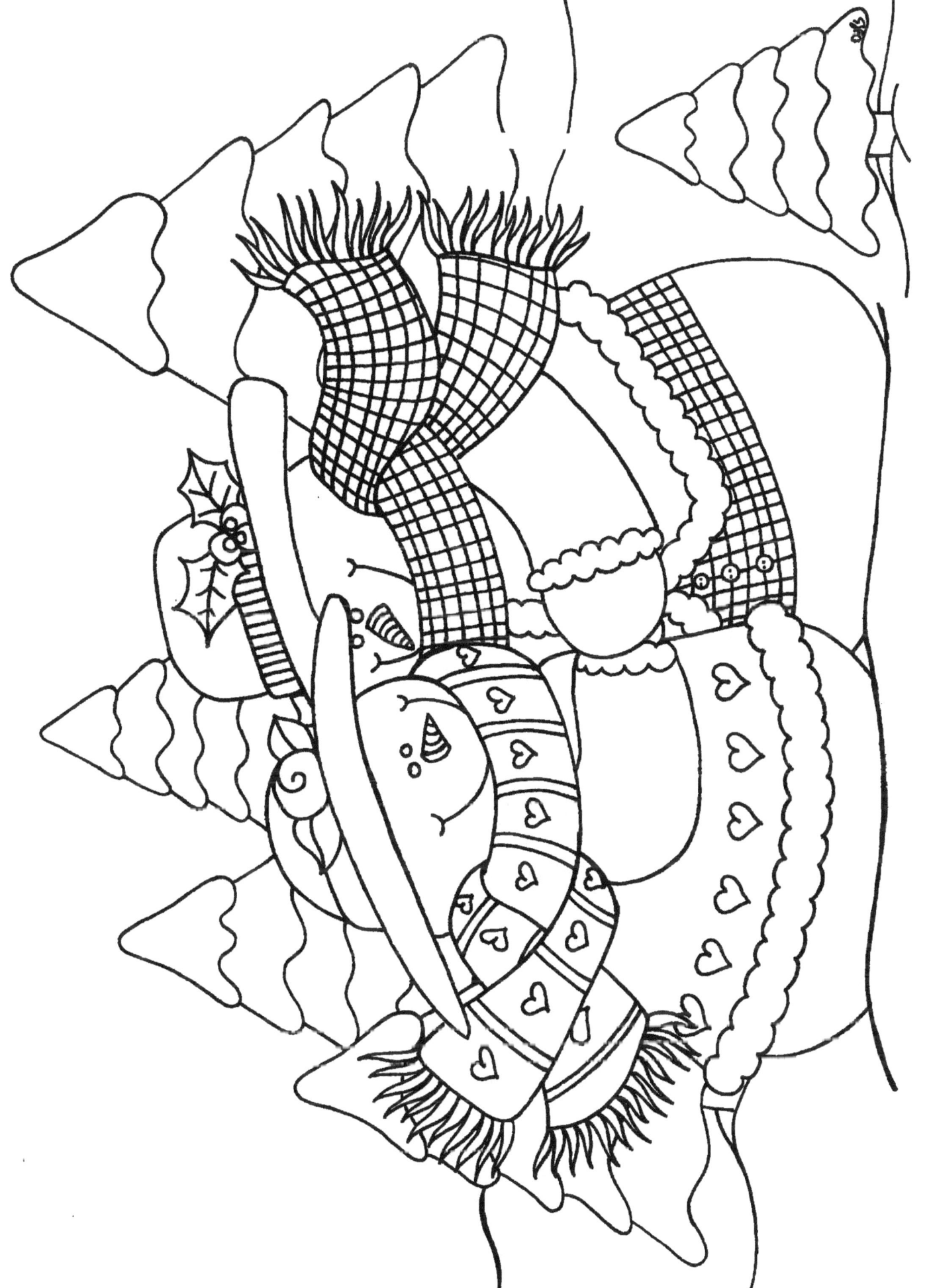

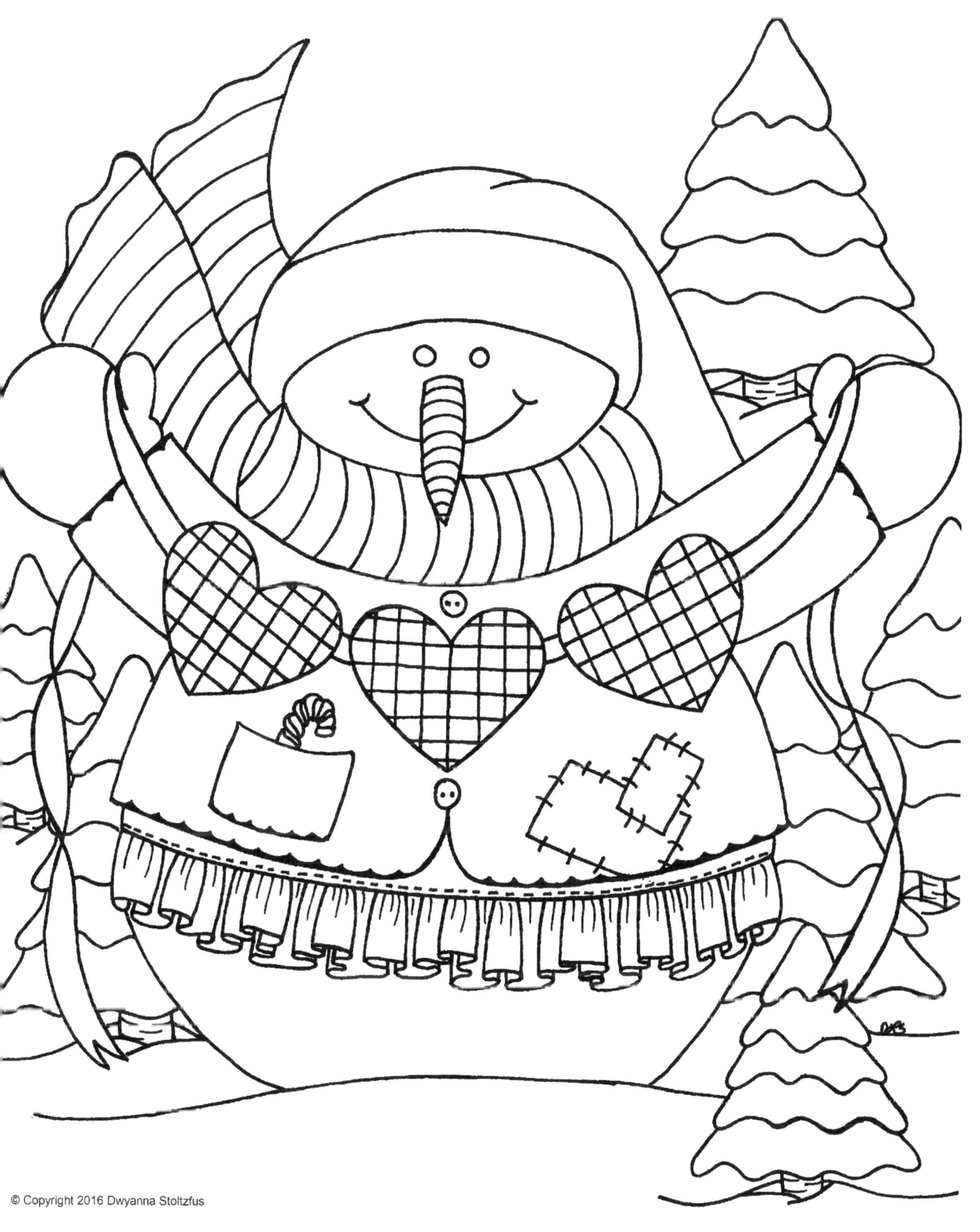

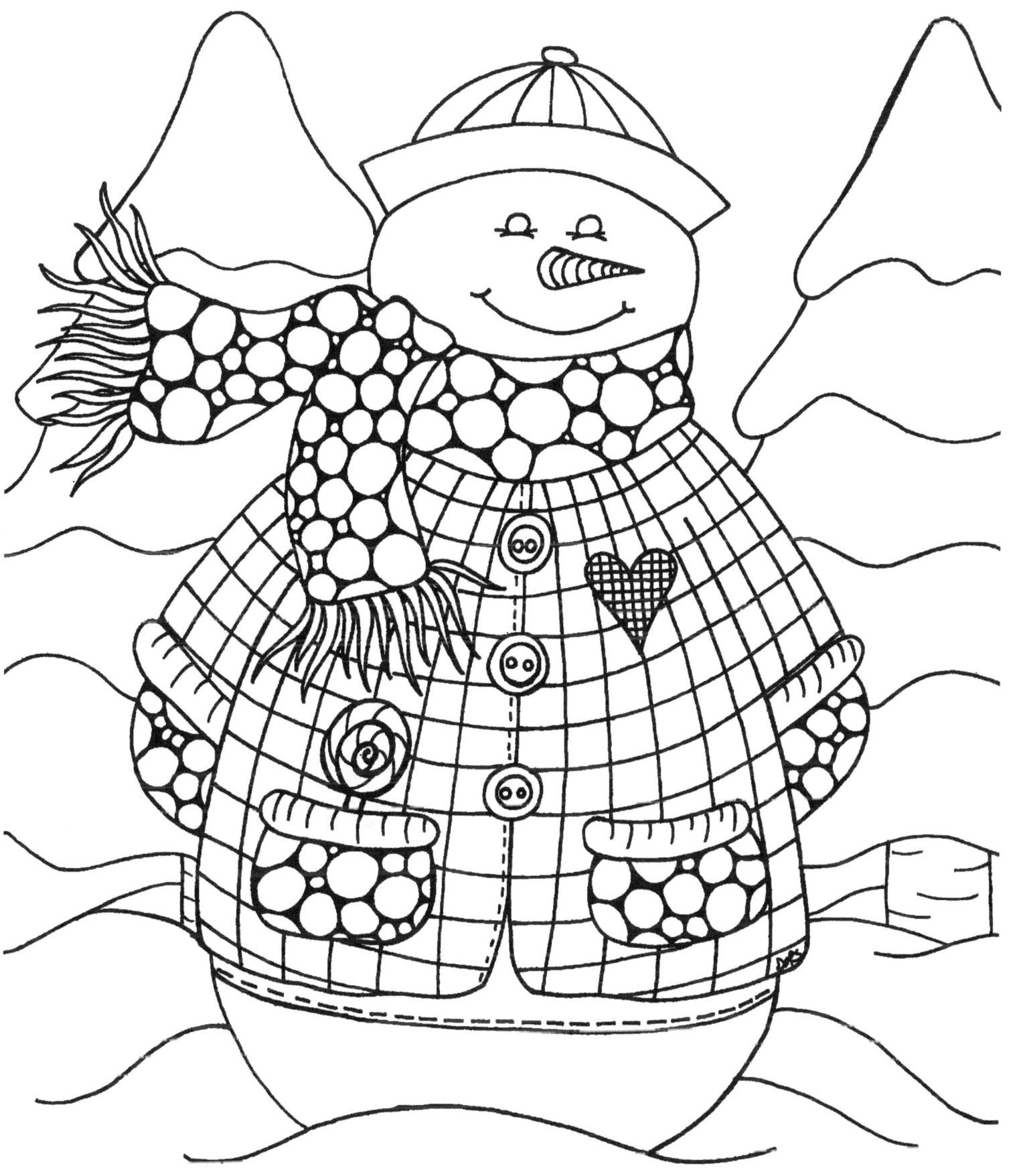

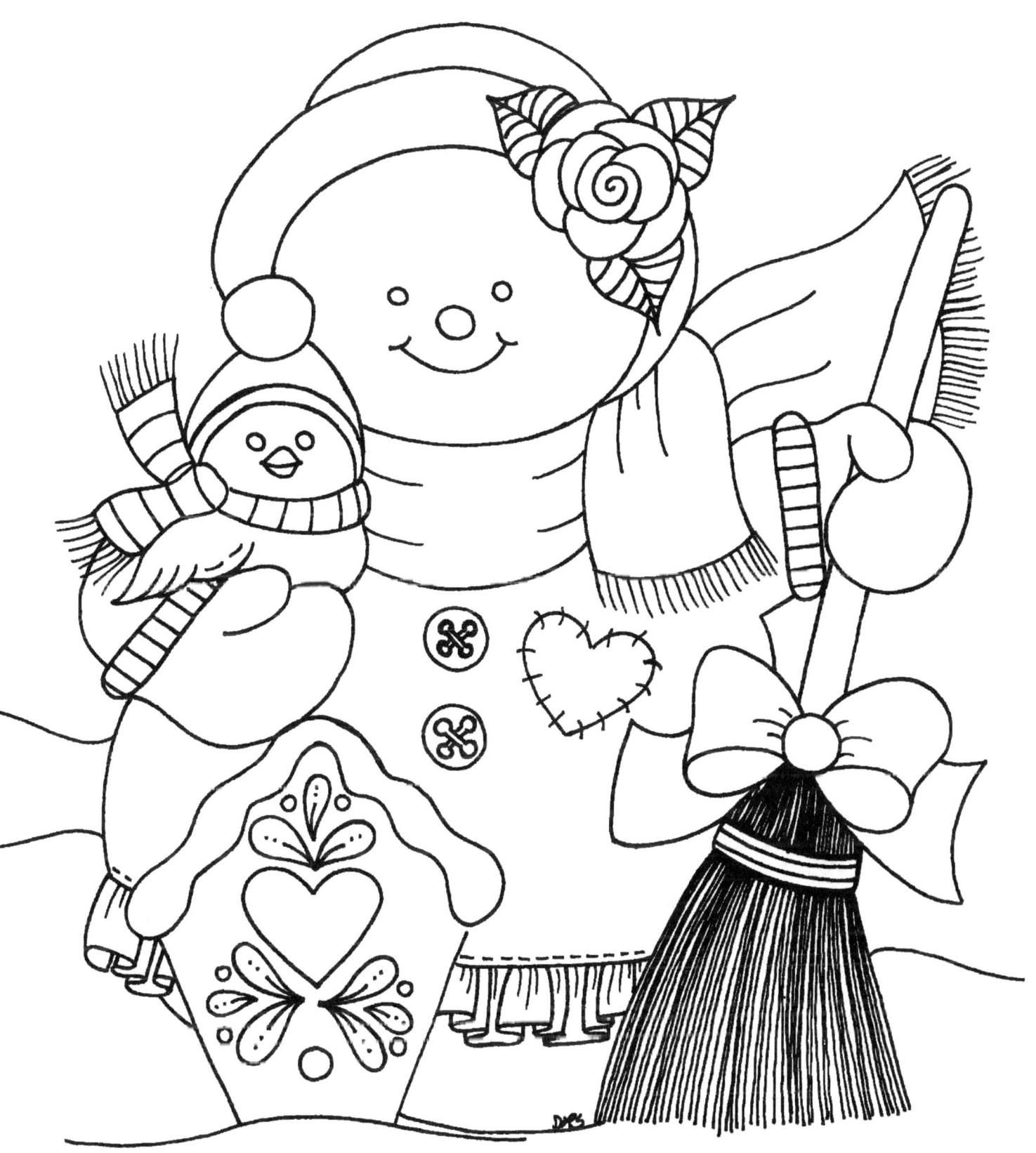

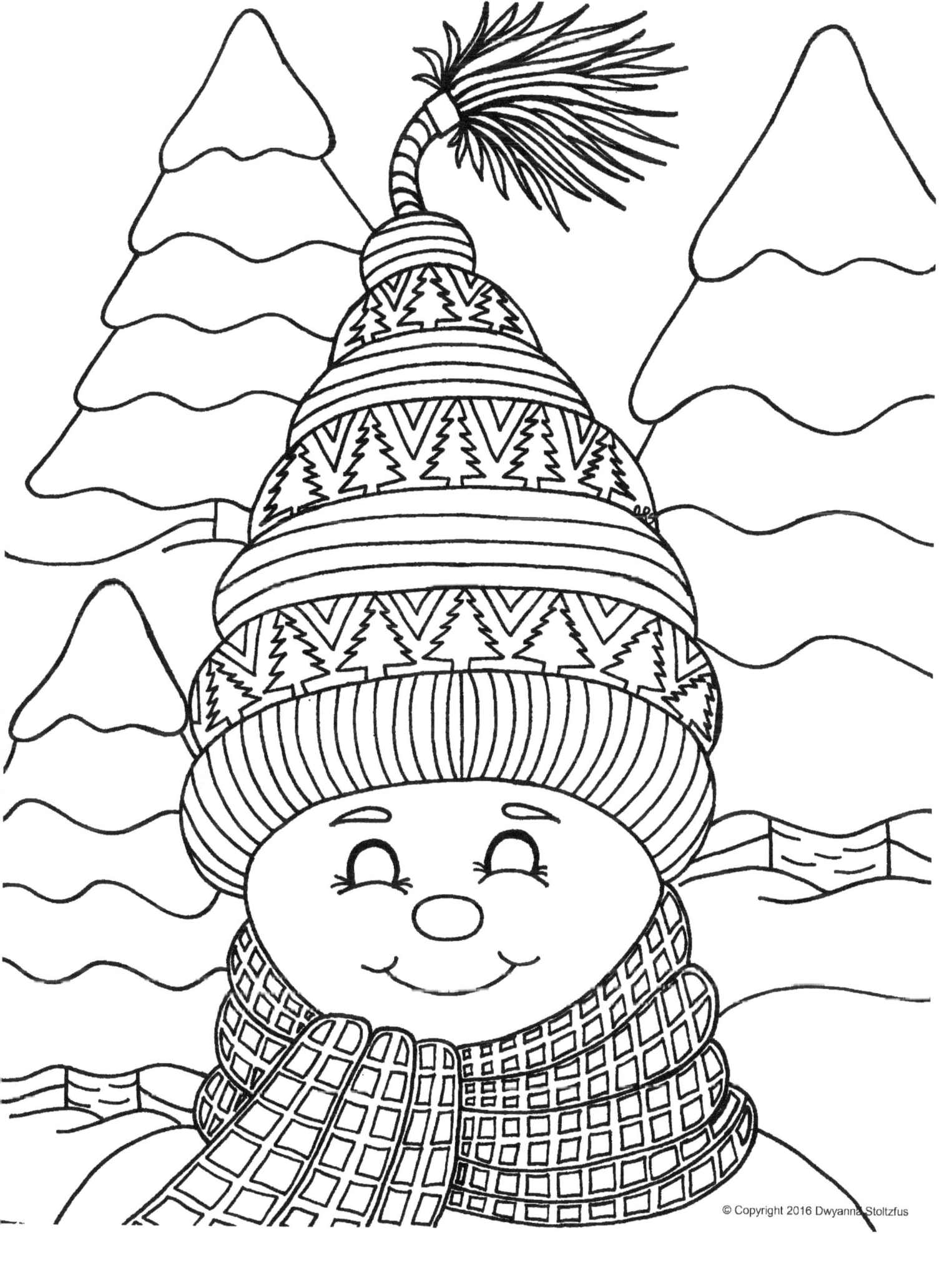

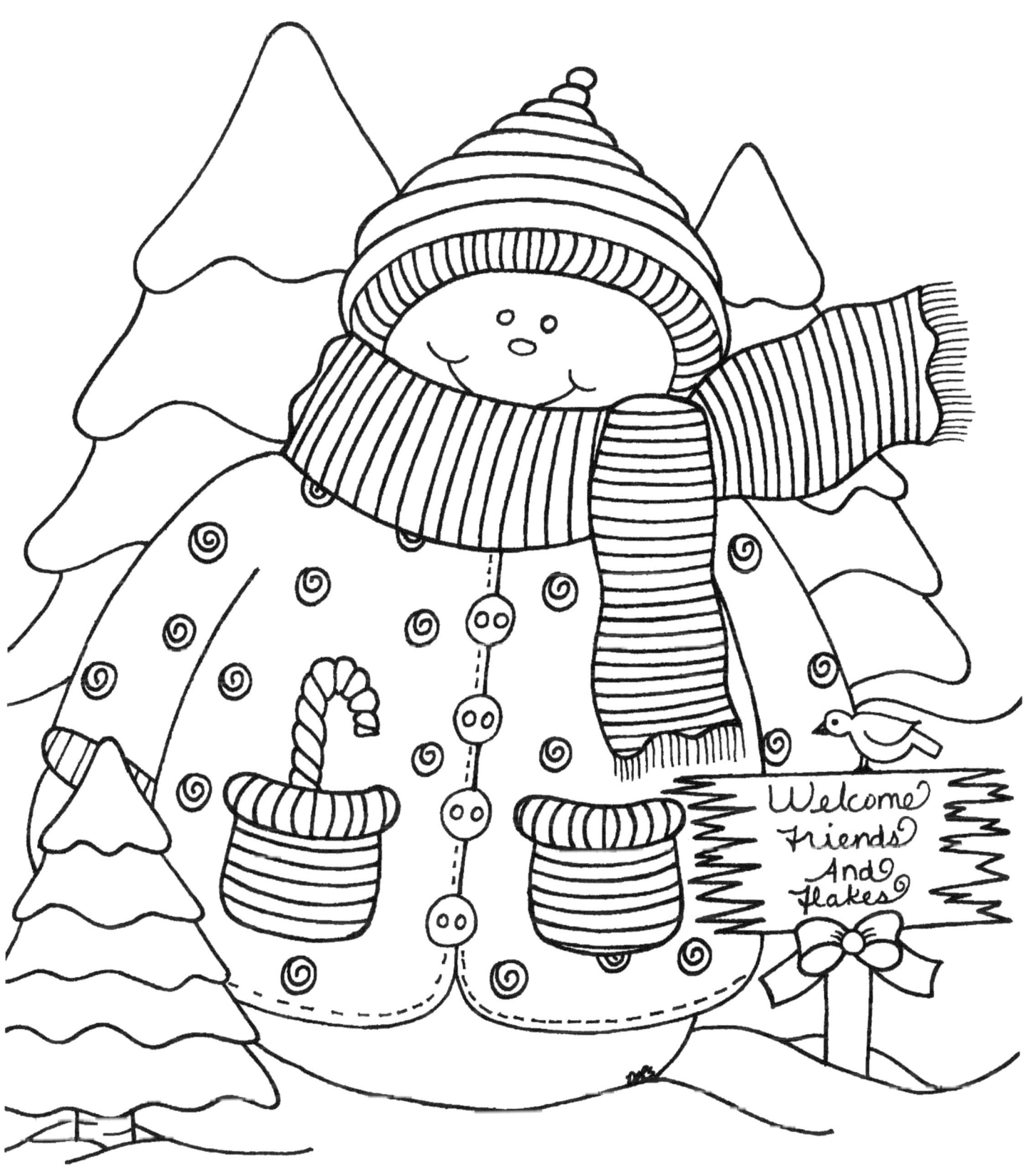

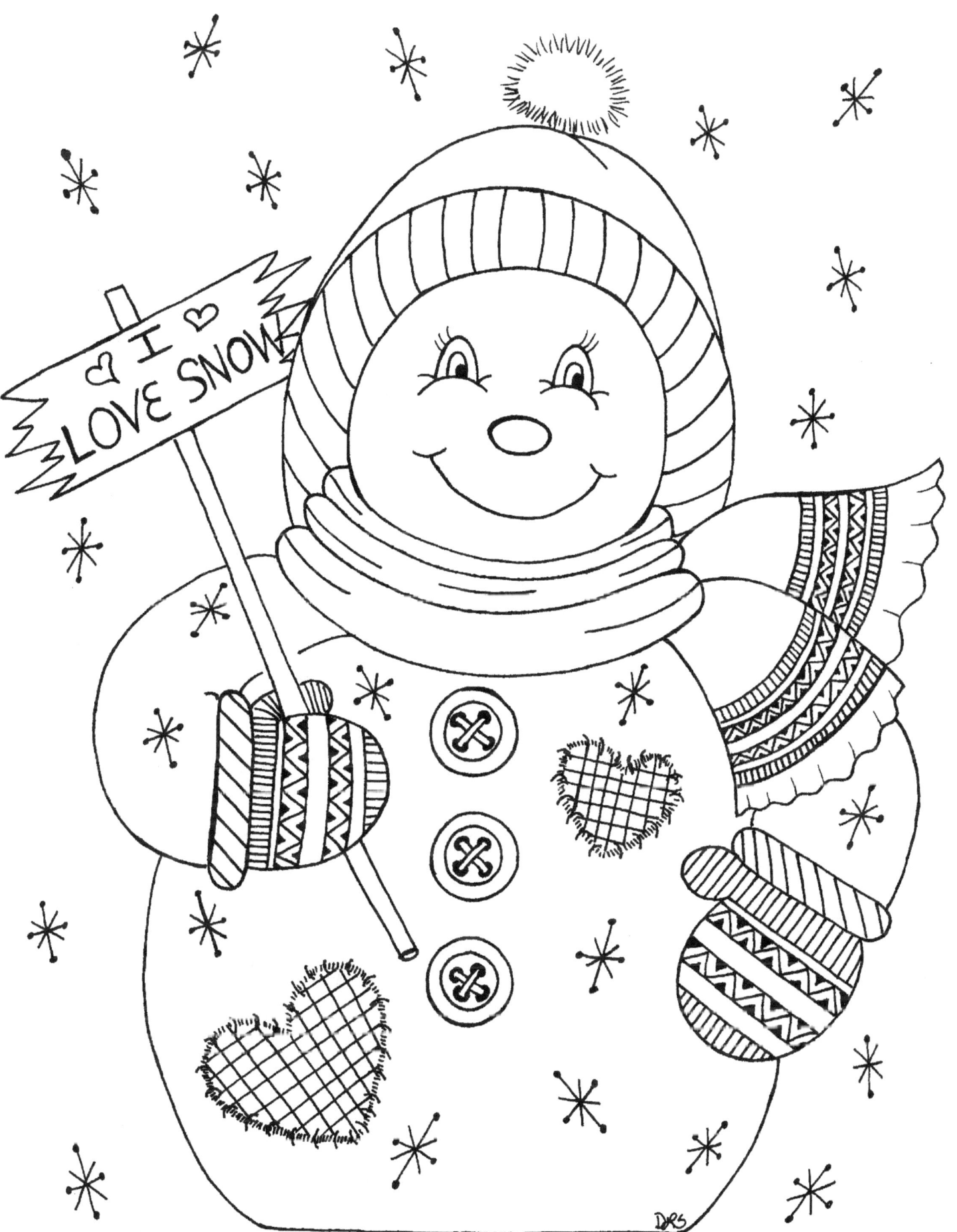

I ♥ LOVE SNOW

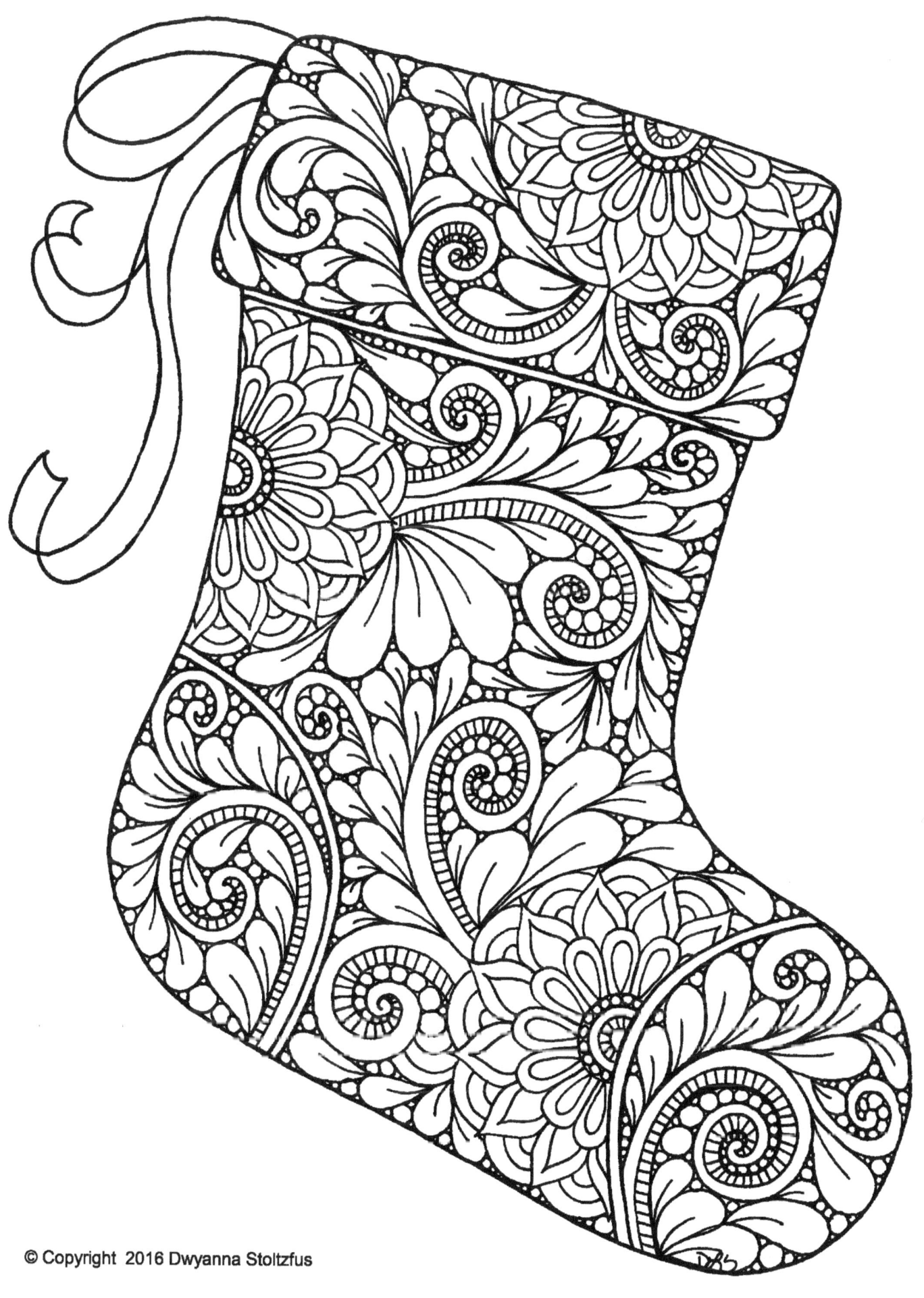

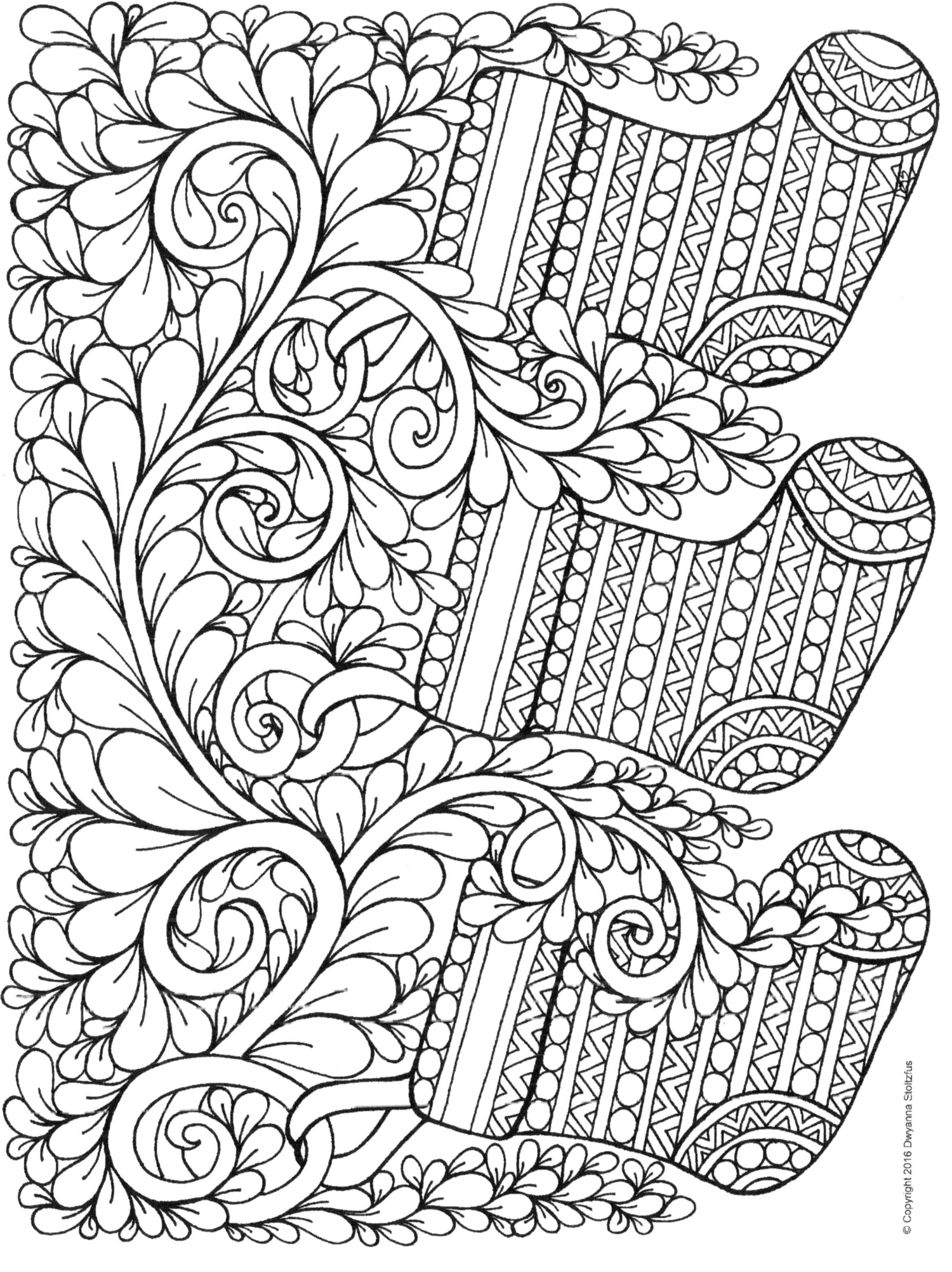

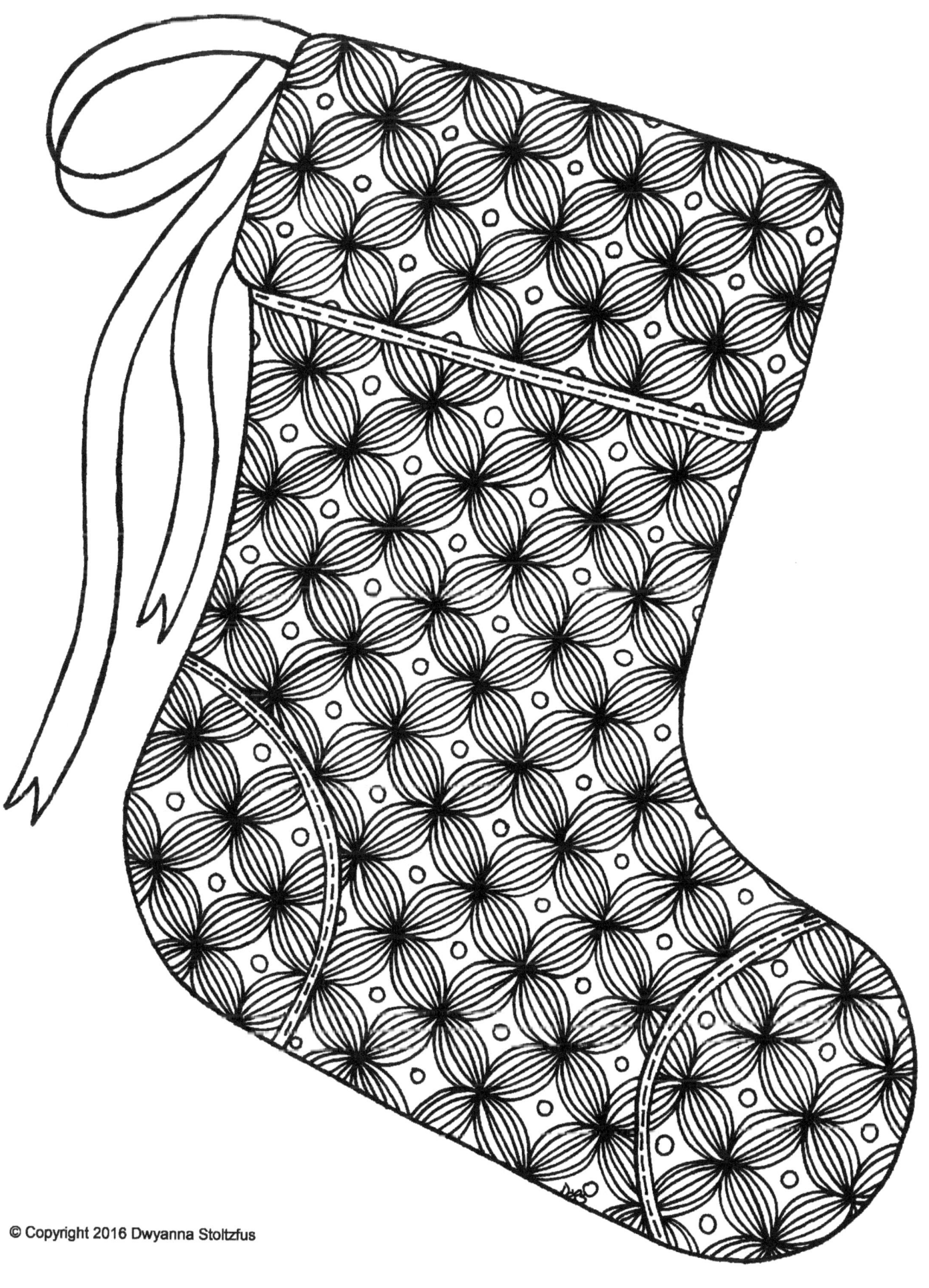

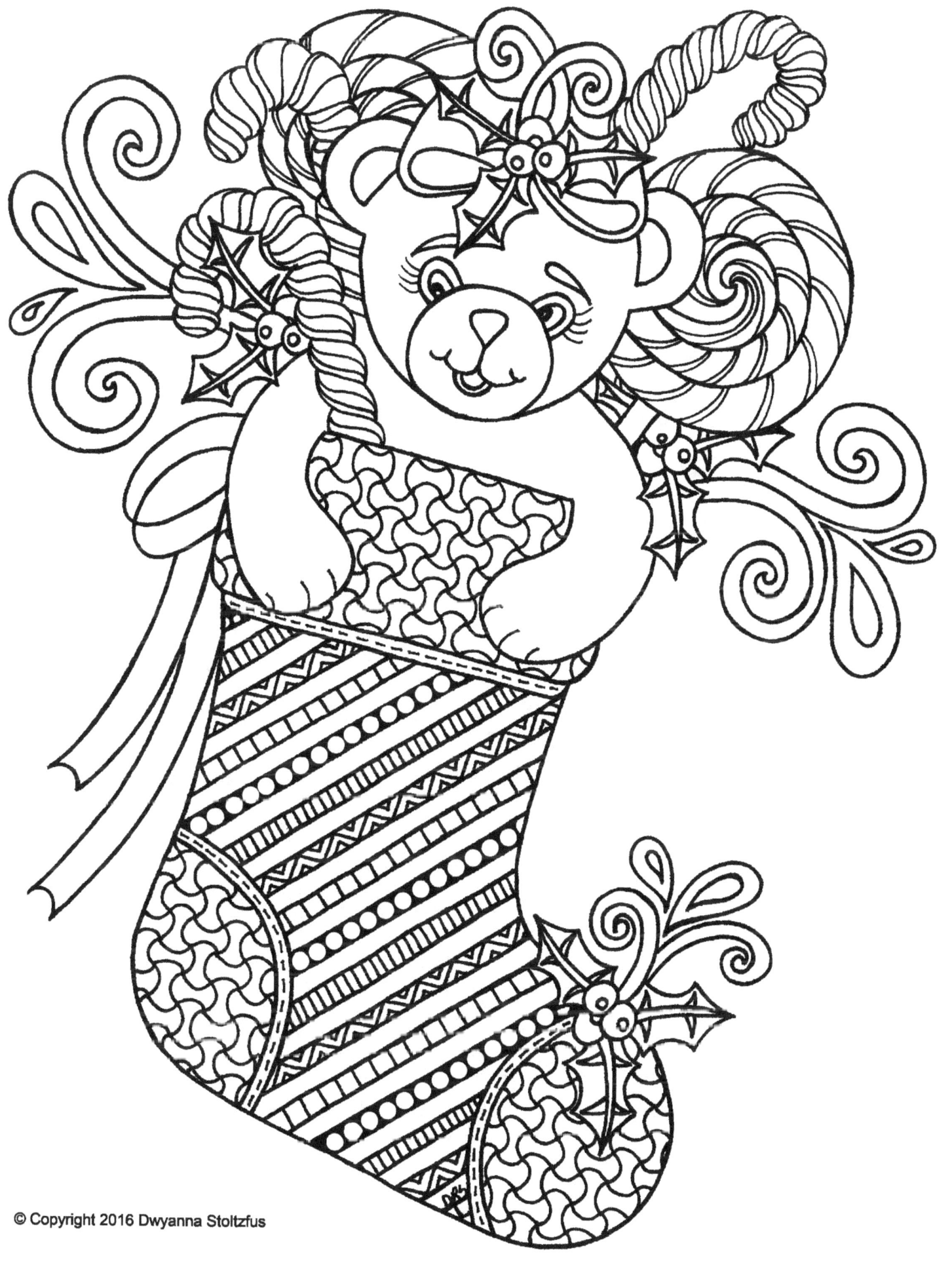

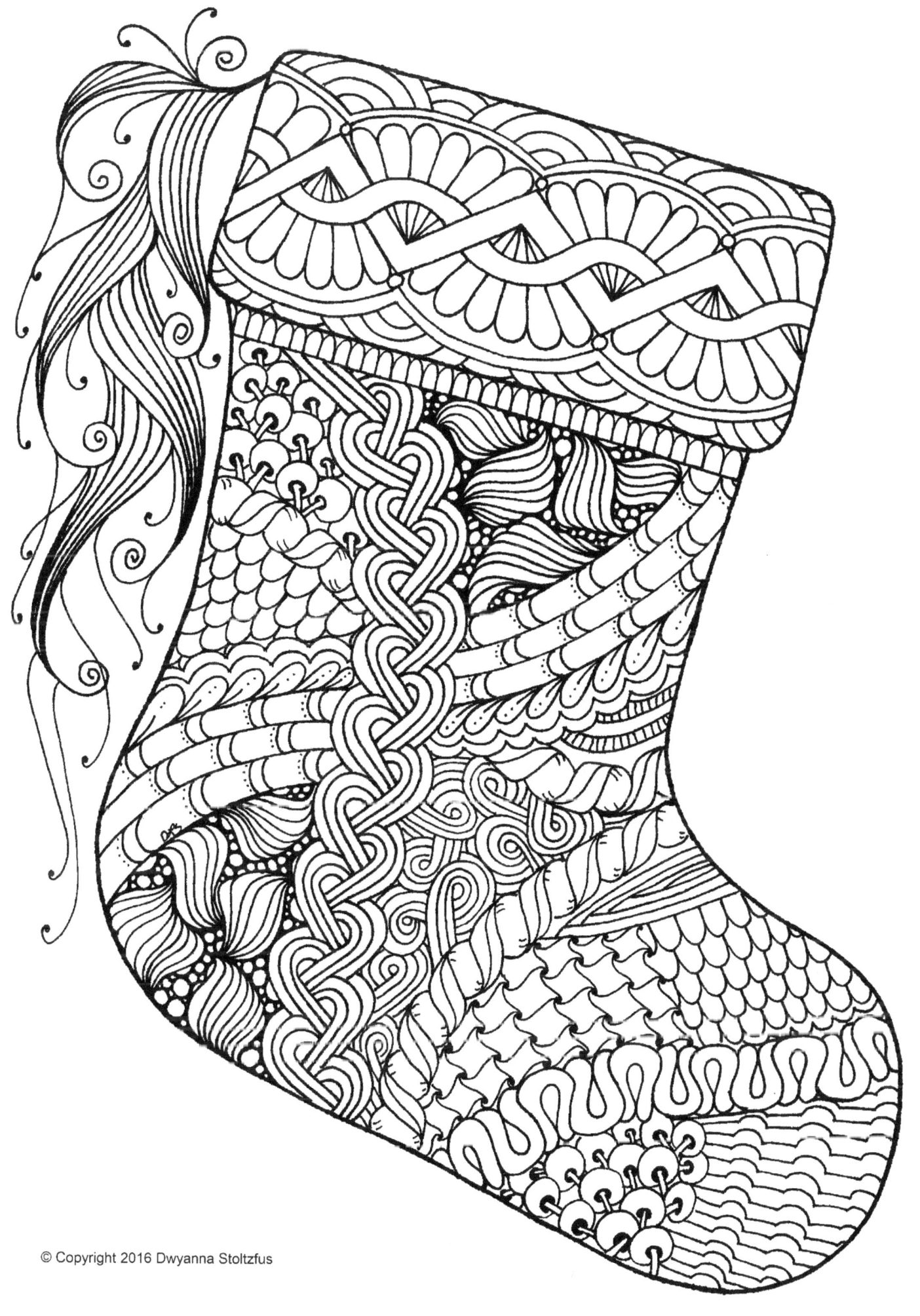

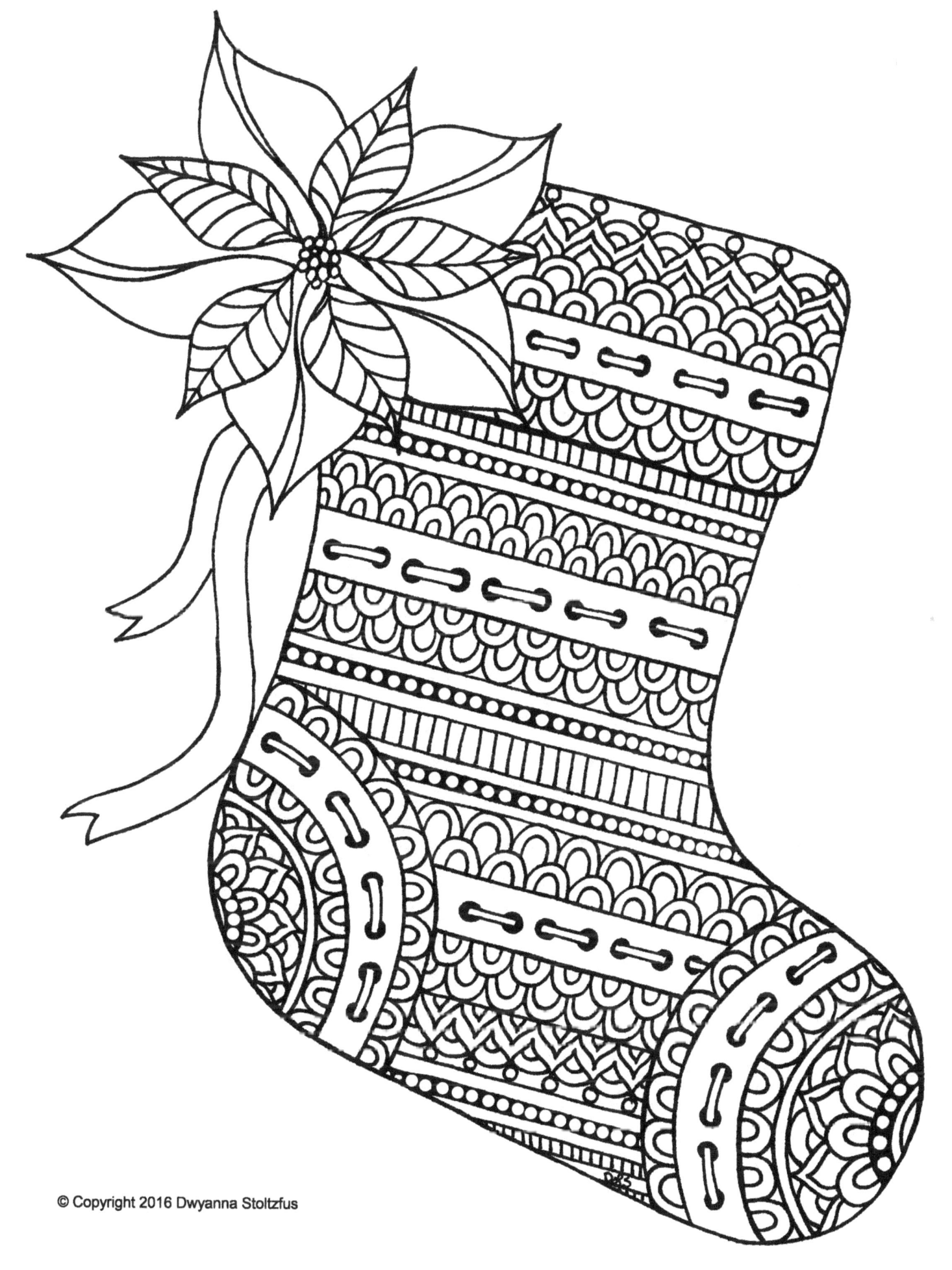

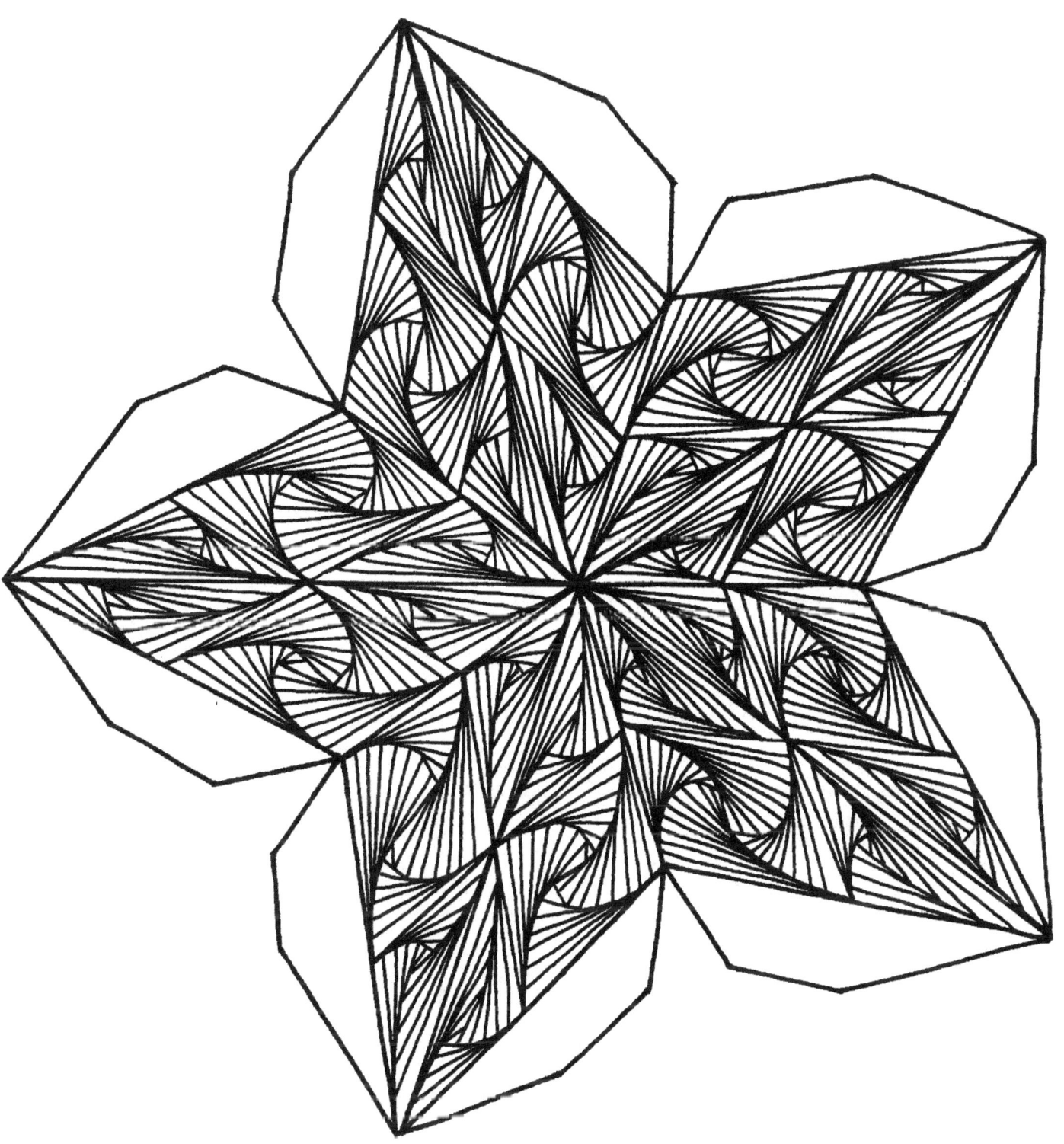

Instructions:
1. Color the star.
2. Cut the star out.
3. Fold the tabs under.
4. Fold the sides of each point downwards.
5. Add a string by pulling a threaded needle through the top of the star.

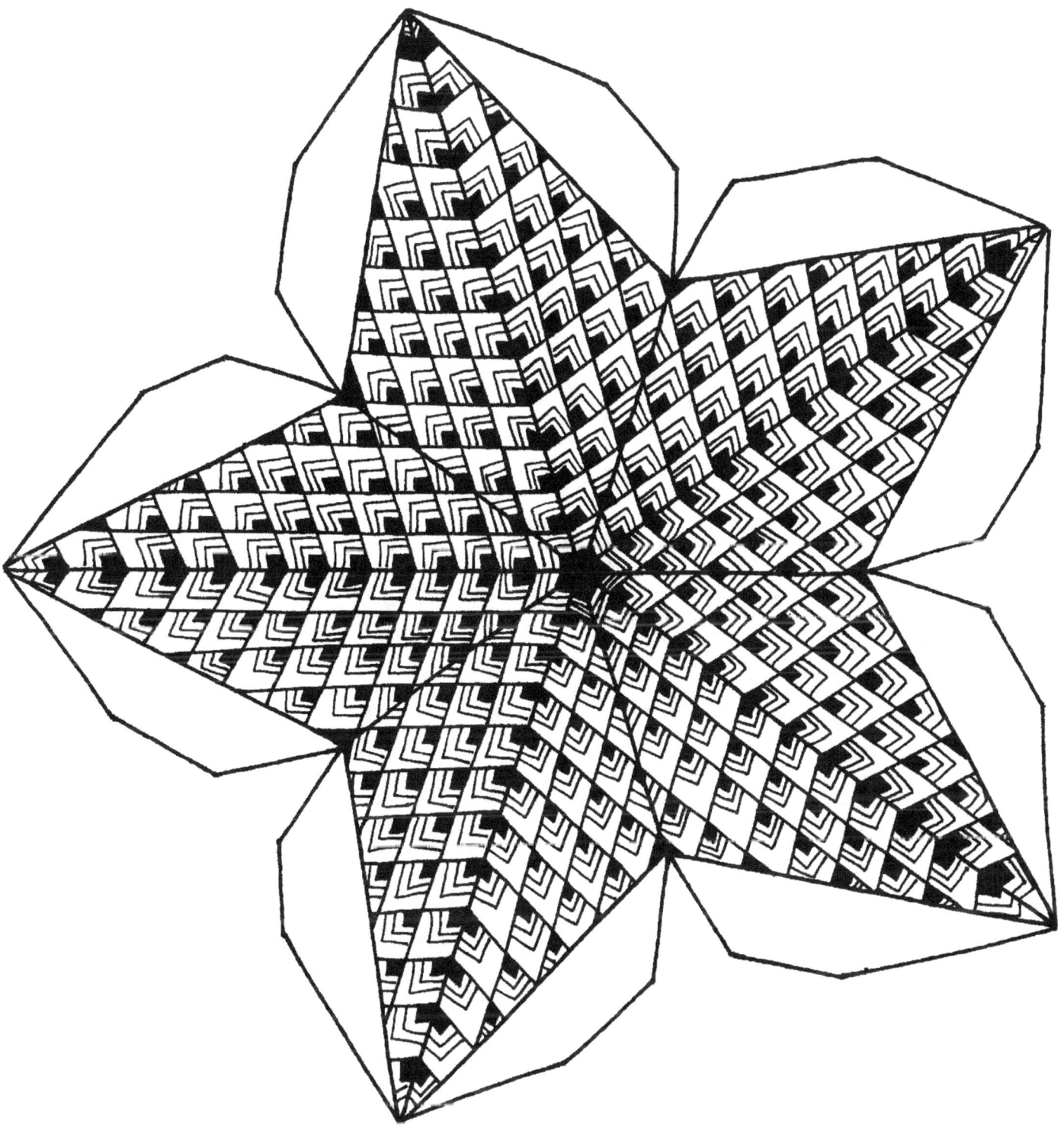

Instructions.
1. Color the star.
2. Cut the star out.
3. Fold the tabs under.
4. Fold the sides of each point downwards.
5. Add a string by pulling a threaded needle through the top of the star.

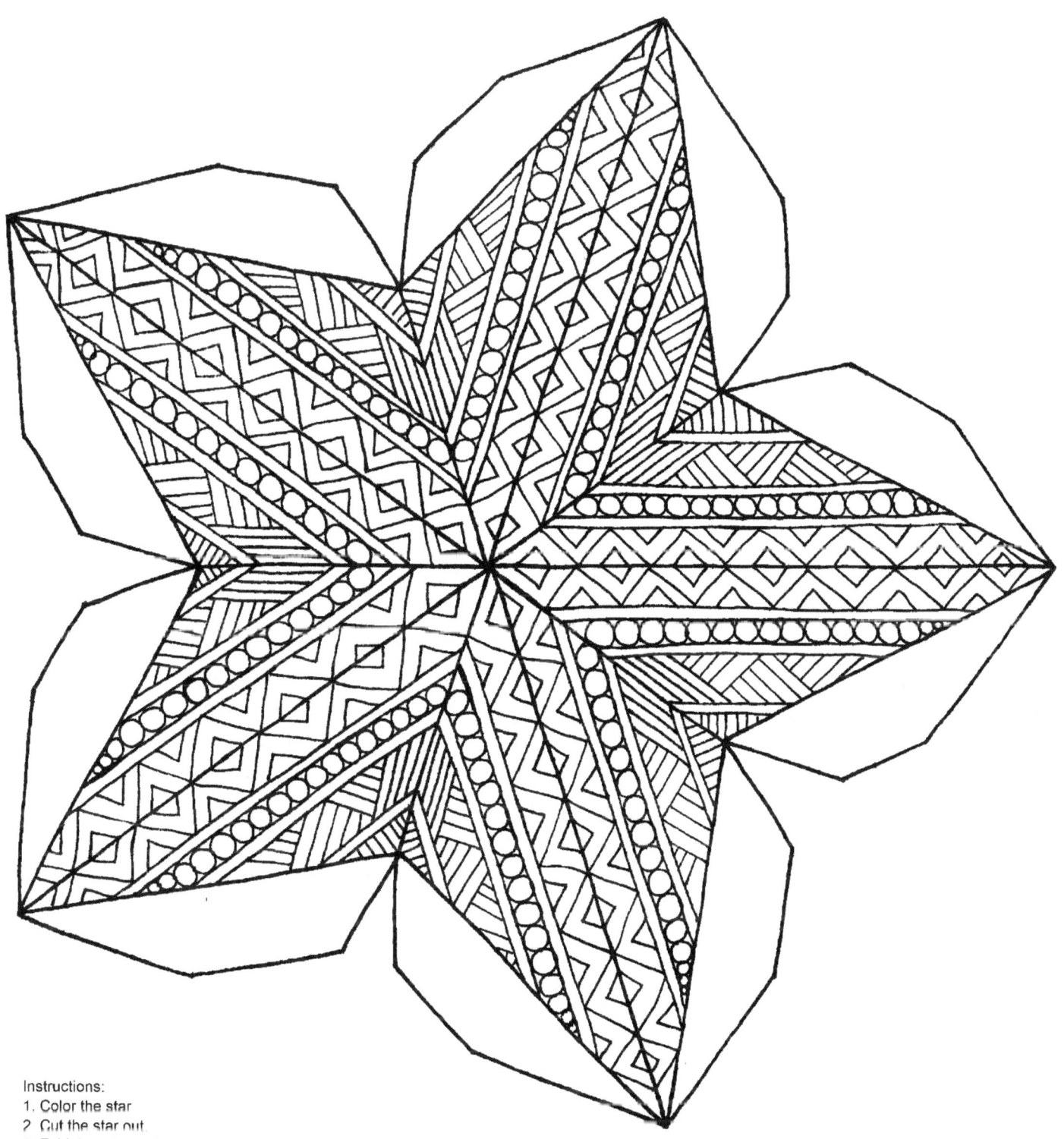

Instructions:
1. Color the star
2. Cut the star out.
3. Fold the tabs under
4. Fold the sides of each point downwards.
5. Add a string by pulling a threaded needle through the top of the star.

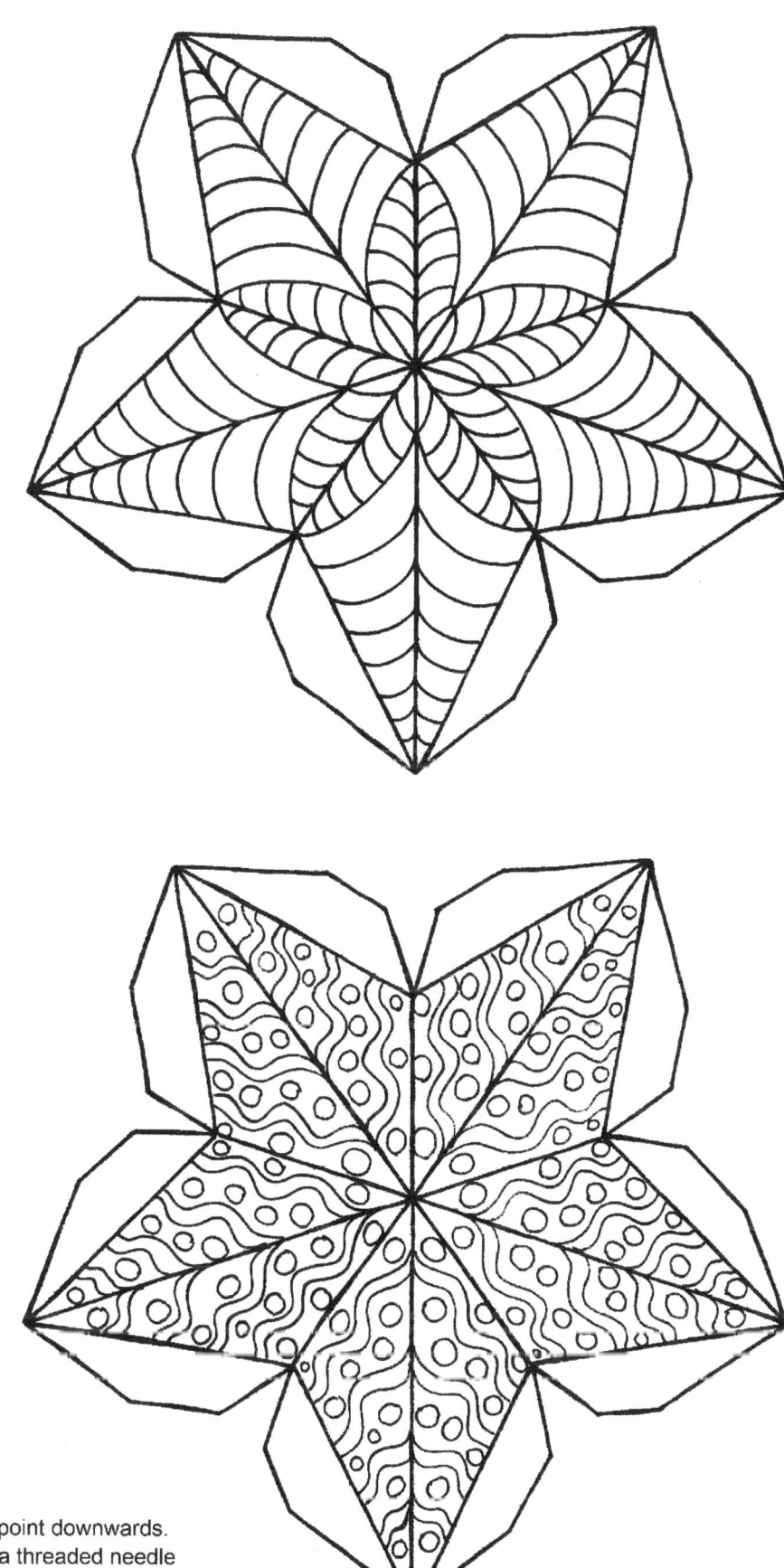

Instructions:
1. Color the star.
2. Cut the star out.
3. Fold the tabs under.
4. Fold the sides of each point downwards.
5. Add a string by pulling a threaded needle through the top of the star.

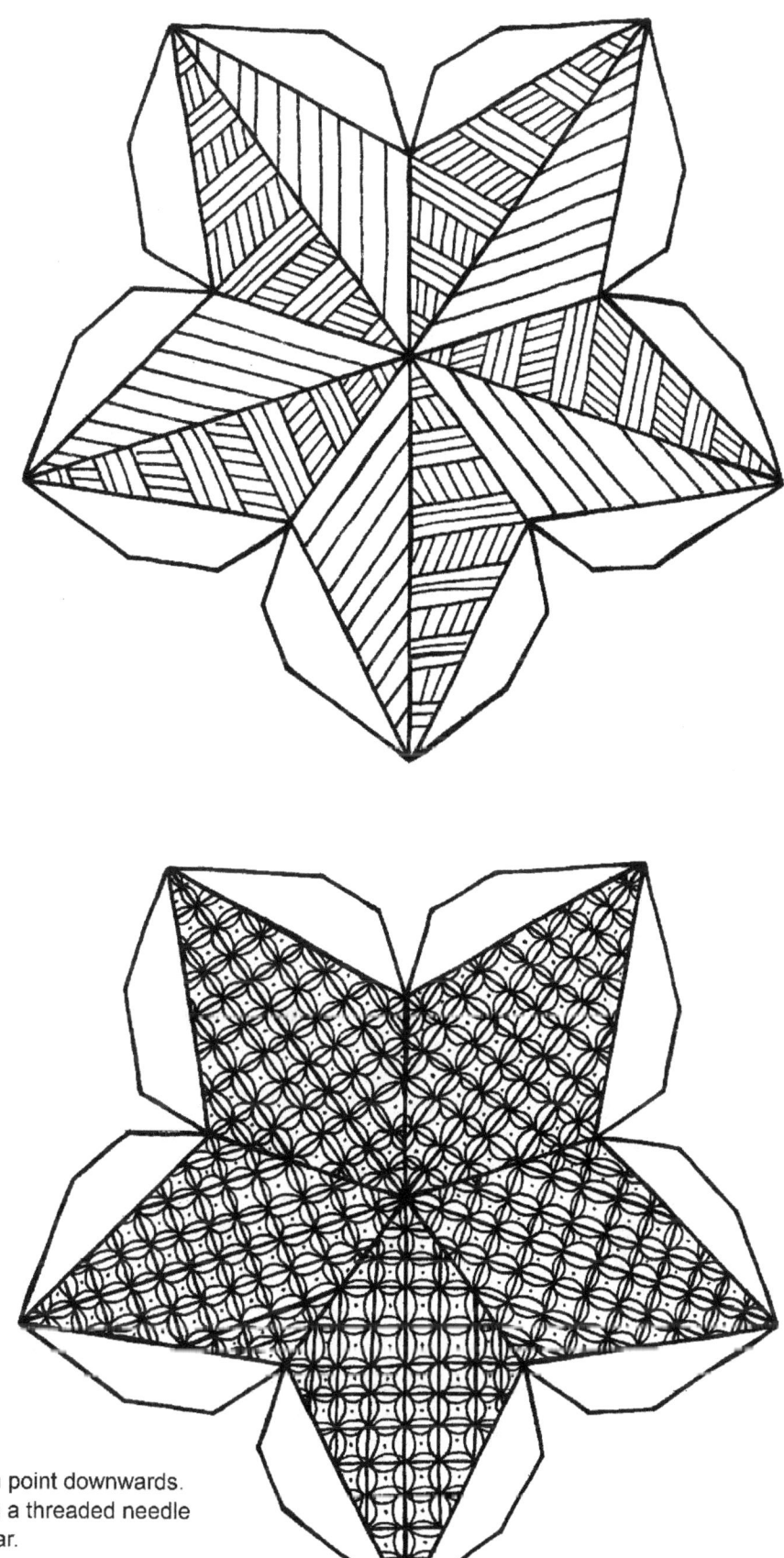

Instructions:
1. Color the star.
2. Cut the star out.
3. Fold the tabs under.
4. Fold the sides of each point downwards.
5. Add a string by pulling a threaded needle through the top of the star.

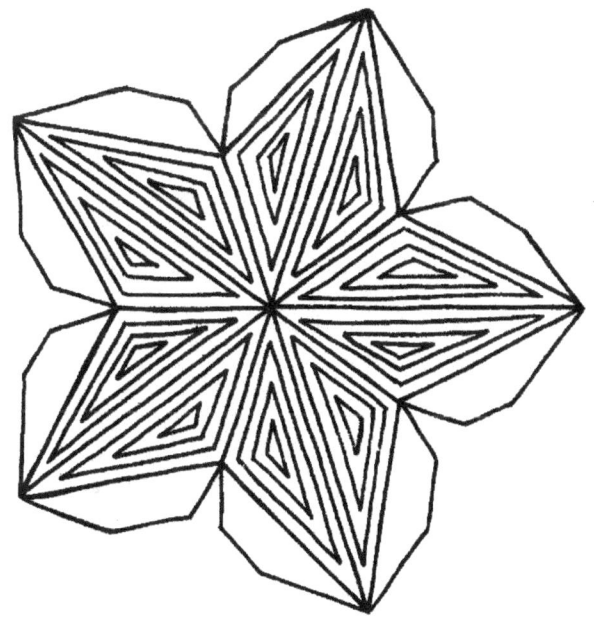
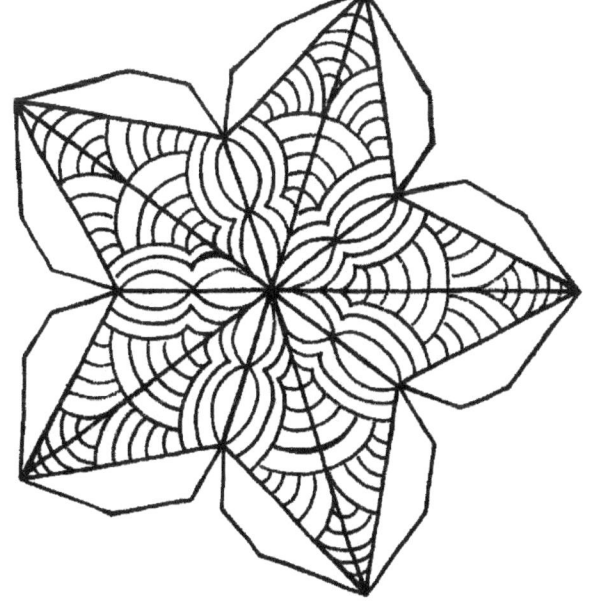
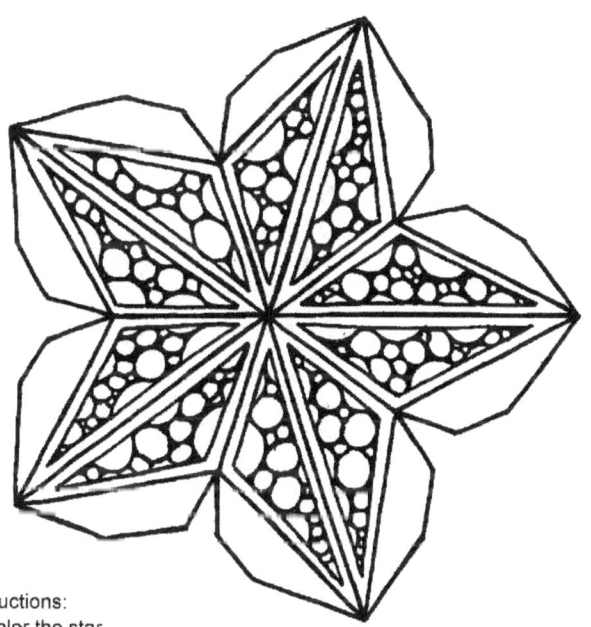
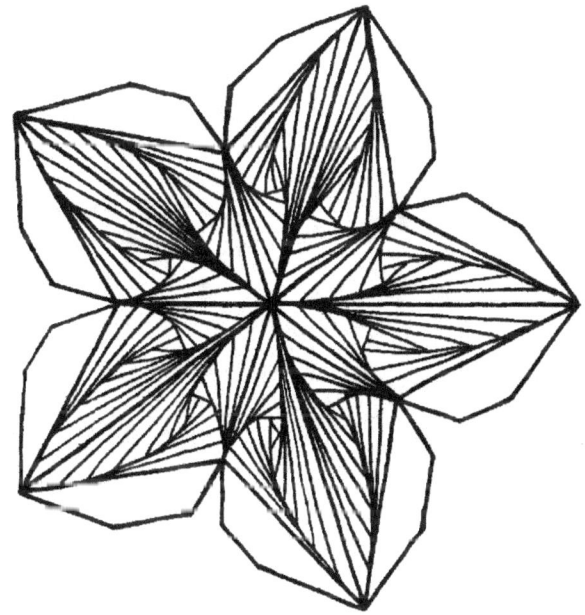

Instructions:
1. Color the star.
2. Cut the star out.
3. Fold the tabs under.
4. Fold the sides of each point downwards.
5. Add a string by pulling a threaded needle through the top of the star.

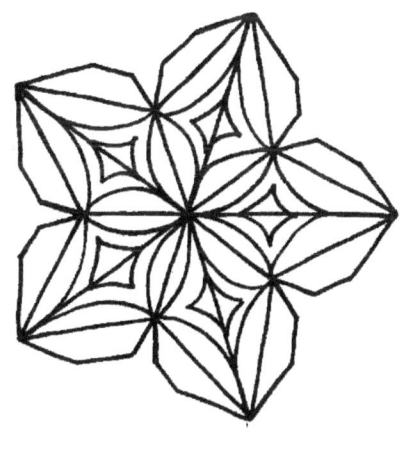 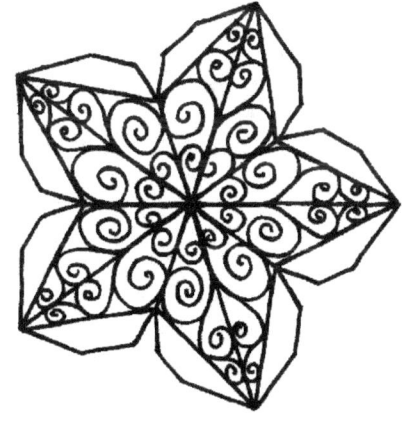 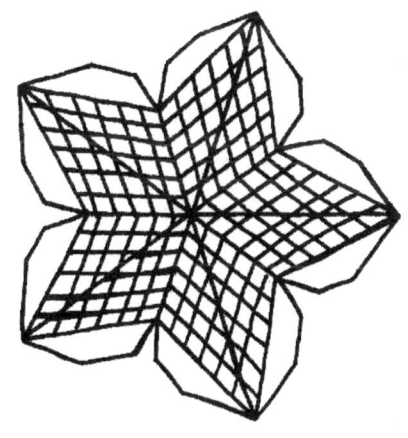

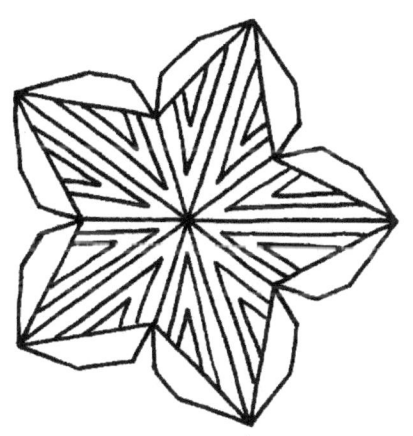 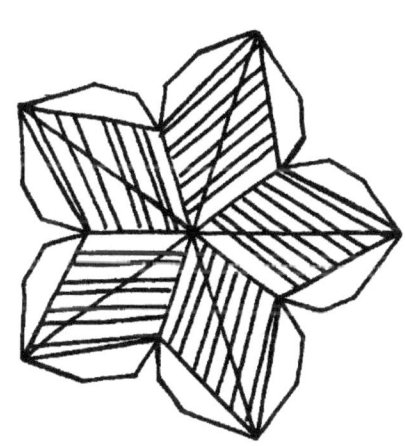 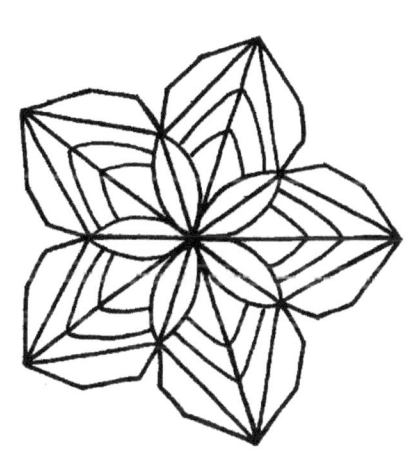

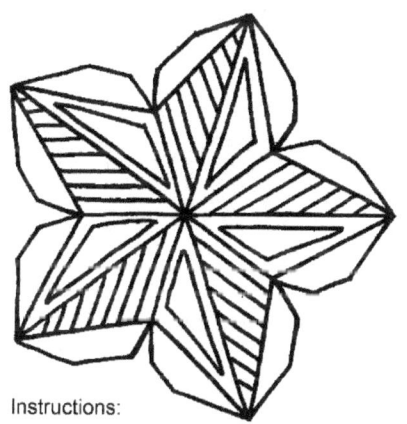 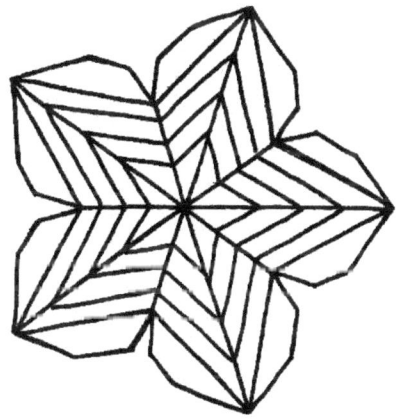 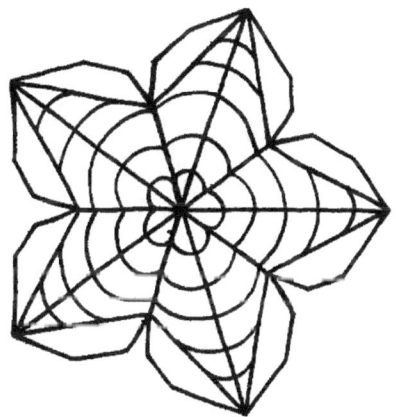

Instructions:
1. Color the star.
2. Cut the star out.
3. Fold the tabs under.
4. Fold the sides of each point downwards.
5. Add a string by pulling a threaded needle through the top of the star.